UNPROFITABLE SERVANTS

Conferences on Humility

By

FR. NIVARD KINSELLA, O.C.S.O.

DUBLIN

M. H. GILL AND SON LTD.

1960

FIRST PUBLISHED, 1960
REPRINTED, 1961

Permissu :

SUPERIORUM RELIGIOSORUM

Nov. 11, 1959

Nihil Obstat :

JACOBUS O'NEILL, C.C.,
Censor Deputatus

Imprimatur :

JOSEPHUS RODGERS, D.D.,
Episcopus Laonensis

Oct. 20, 1959

© NIVARD KINSELLA, O.C.S.O. 1960.

*Printed and Bound in the Republic of Ireland at the
Press of the Publishers.*

CONTENTS

ACKNOWLEDGEMENT

The substance of this book first appeared as articles in *Sursum Corda*, a spiritual review published monthly by the Franciscan Fathers in Australia (Editorial address: 45, Victoria St., Waverley, New South Wales). Acknowledgement is here made to the Editor for permission to republish.

FOREWORD

THERE IS LITTLE that is new in the following pages. Their justification lies in the fact that while most of what they contain has been said before, it has not been said in a single book. There are several books in English on humility, but the greater number are either translations, or editions of older treatises or else they deal with a particular aspect of the virtue, such as the theology of humility. Our aim here has been to give, in a series of conferences, an adequate and satisfying analysis of the virtue, its importance, its practice and the examples of it given us by the lives of Our Lord and his Mother. Among the saints the greatest example of humility is St. John the Baptist; hence we have included a chapter on him. It may cause some surprise that there is no discussion of the teaching of St. Benedict on the virtue, since he gives it such an important place in his Rule. This omission is deliberate. The place of humility in the monastic ascesis is a subject that cannot be dealt with adequately in a chapter or two—it needs a book to itself. Our concern here is with the virtue as such, apart from its special place in monastic spirituality. There is need, it seems, for a treatment of the virtue of humility that is modern in idiom and approach, restating the unchanging principles about it, and answering the genuine difficulties and problems that its practice seems to give rise to in the minds of some. This book is an attempt to meet that need.

Mount St. Joseph Abbey,
Roscrea

CHAPTER I

" *WHAT HAVE YOU THAT YOU HAVE NOT RECEIVED?* "

H UMILITY is a difficult virtue—difficult to get clear ideas on as well as difficult to acquire. Its nature is such that we can hardly satisfy ourselves that we have it and leave it at that, although some of the saints have done so. Those who have it are usually unaware of the fact, and the very realisation that you are lacking in it, is itself a degree of the virtue. You may have it and have few of its outward signs. On the other hand you may appear humble without really being so in fact. You may stand with the Publican afar off and yet be proud that you are not a Pharisee. When present in another person humility is easily confused with weakness, or with a particular kind of temperament. If we ourselves happen to possess it, we may have fears about it because of disturbing affinities we imagine it to have with inferiority complexes and self-deprecia-tion. " Humility is one of the most difficult virtues to attain and to ascertain. It lies close upon the heart itself, and its tests are exceedingly delicate and subtle. Its counterfeits abound." (Newman).

All that being so, it might appear best to leave the matter and not probe too deeply into it. After all, the virtues grow simul-taneously, like the fingers of a hand. If we have charity, we will also have humility. So why worry about the theory of it?

Some of the saints go into it at great length, giving degrees of the virtue, and marking progress in it by steps and grades. But if we examine their teaching we find that their degrees of humility are really degrees of the spiritual life. Therefore if our general spiritual health is sound, there can be nothing wrong with our humility. We can afford to forget it in practice. It will look after itself. Such an attitude would be a pity—for it is very much the ostrich head-in-the-sand attitude. You can take things for granted for so long. Then something goes wrong and you are faced with a crisis. If a crack appears in the wall of a building, and you decide to renew the roof-trusses because you have always taken the foundations for granted, you are liable to have more cracks appearing pretty soon.

Besides, pride is such an insidious vice. It insinuates itself even into our best actions if we do not take care. There is nothing we cannot be proud of—even of our progress in humility. In everything we do pride is liable to appear—or at least to be there, even if it does not manifest itself. Pride brought Lucifer down; pride caused the sin of Adam. And both Adam and Lucifer were very much stronger than we are.

Perhaps part of the difficulty about humility comes from its all-pervasiveness in the spiritual life. We said that pride can insinuate itself into everything we do. The fact is that our every act will be coloured either by pride or by humility. In everything you do, you will act either as a proud or as a humble man. There is no alternative in practice—even in your acts of virtue. Humility, therefore, has as many possible ramifications as pride, and consequently as many facets. Its practice may lead a man to deprecate praise, to evade the limelight, to be tolerant and kind towards another, to speak of his unworthiness, to smile at a rebuff or a slight, or even at what appears to be disaster. Yet humility in itself is none of these things. It is something very simple; it is a realisation of our creaturehood—a true knowledge of ourselves in relation to God.

Where then are our ideas—or better perhaps call them imaginings —of the humble man as a miserable sort of fellow who allows himself to be used as a door-mat by everyone, who goes about denying the existence of his obvious gifts, natural and supernatural, and who is never happy unless people despise him? Perhaps we are taking the fruit for the tree, owing to our putting too much emphasis on the graces or attractions of a particular saint. Possibly too what we think to be the fruit of the virtue is really the fruit of our imagination. Further, we are probably identifying the means with the end. All spiritual writers talk about humility. Many of them do not analyse it, but simply give rules and practices for acquiring it. These latter are not humility, but acts of various other virtues that will lead to humility. We should not identify them with humility, but we often do so. At all events, whatever the reason for our misunderstanding, the fact remains that humility is nothing more or less than the attitude of the creature in presence of his Creator, and the way of acting which results from such an attitude.

It is important to be convinced of this. Pride was the sin of Adam, who desired to be as a god knowing good and evil. Every sin of pride is a repetition of that scene in the garden. We would be as gods—we would be sufficient unto ourselves, we would be our own law, our own strength, our own virtue, we would do without God. Perhaps it may not appear quite as openly as that but what else is it at root? Pride is the excessive desire of our own excellence. It might be clearer if we used the word love instead of desire. And because of original sin, because of the darkness that has come upon our intellect, we are most prone to pride. We tend to misunderstand that freedom which is God's greatest gift to us, and to regard it as complete autonomy. As though we were completely sufficient unto ourselves and could find in ourselves the beginning and end of all our actions. What else in fact are we doing when we refer any good to ourselves, or when we ignore God and commit sin?

The truth is just the opposite—that we are completely dependent. In everything we are and in everything we do we depend on God, whether in the natural order or in that of grace. Of ourselves we have nothing and we are nothing. We are left with only one thing which we can call our own, our sin, which is itself a nothingness, a negation, a deprival of good. We depend on God so fully and so completely that if for a single moment he left us to ourselves, we would cease to exist. As Father Trese puts it in one of his books, we would disappear so completely and effectively that even God himself could not find us if he looked for us afterwards. It is not that we would die, or wither away spiritually. We would simply vanish, body and soul. We would no longer be—for in him we live and move and are. Without him there is nothing.

In him we are. Did we come into being of ourselves, or had we any say in or control over the matter? God created us. And did he then leave us to our own devices? Did he, once we had begun to be, leave us to ourselves as one might wind up a clock and leave it? Not at all—his creation goes on all the time. We live continually in the shadow of his hand. Without him we could not be. For on him, on his conserving power, we depend for every moment of our lives and for everything we do. Without his continued presence we could not be. Just as God gave us the first moment of existence, so he must give us every moment. We are as dependent on him for each instance of life as we were for the first. That is why we say that creation goes on all the time. Each passing instant is no different from the one that went before, the second is no different from the first—each one must come to us from God. We are never so independent that we suffice to keep ourselves in being, no more than we sufficed to bring ourselves into being. It might come home to us better if we reflected that without him we could not speak or think. Without his co-operation and assistance I could not write these words and you could not read them.

But in the supernatural order our complete dependence on God is even more marked. He gave us grace and sonship in Adam, but Adam refused the gift because he wanted to be as a god. He made something of himself and found that he was nothing—cast naked with his sin upon the barren earth. But God, who might fairly have ended it all at that, and left us, as Adam begot us, in darkness and in error, set about repairing the ruin. He sent a new Adam, his Son, who by his sufferings and death would restore us and all things in himself. And so to all who believe in him, he gives once more the power to become the sons of God. Great as was the first creation, the remaking is more wonderful still.

And this remaking, this refashioning of us, which is the Redemption, takes place only by incorporation into Christ. We are grafted onto him, so that we no longer live with our own life but with his. We are no longer alone, small, helpless—we are one body with him, a new creature, branches of the heavenly vine, planted by the almighty vine-dresser.

There is no possibility here of independent life. Such independence does not exist in the scheme of things. We are Christ's or we are nothing. We live in his Mystical Body or we die. We live by him or we do not live at all—for without him we can do nothing. This admits of no exception or qualification. We cannot even pronounce the name of Jesus without his helping grace. He said quite simply and absolutely: You can do nothing. What we do in him is living and vital and will live forever; what is done outside of him, without him, is empty and hollow and dead.

How then can we justify an undue self-esteem? What have we that we have not received? And if we have received, why do we glory as if we had not? How can any other attitude be right than that of the poor man in the gospel who was cured and ran after

Our Lord glorifying God? For we have not merely been cured—
we have been made, and then re-made and that supernaturally.
When we failed in Adam we were given a greater than Adam. He
would not leave us just creatures—he would make us sons. And
lest we be tempted to think it cost him nothing, he endured
the cross. God so loved me that he became man, suffered and died
for me—how often we have heard the words and how little they
can come to mean! Yet how great the truth that they contain!
Not that he raised us poor, from the filth, to sit with the princes
of his people (Cf. *Ps.* 112). But that he took the filth, the slime
of the earth, and breathed into it a living soul and made that soul
his son.

" And then," Juliana of Norwich tells us, "I saw a little thing,
about the size of a hazel nut, in the palm of my hand . . . and I
looked at it and thought: What may this be? And it was answered:
It is all that was made. And I marvelled that it should last, for I
thought it might have fallen away to nothing it was so little. And
I was answered: It lasts and will ever last because God loves it.
So all things have being by the love of God."

If we reflected upon ourselves we should marvel that we last
and do not rather fall away to nothingness, we are so little. In him
we are. We, like all else, have being because God loves us. To
desire our own excellence then is to love something that is not.
To be proud is to be an idolator . . . but the idol is something
that really is not. Worse than the idolatry of the Israelites before
the golden calf, our idolatry is a bowing down before a thing of
our imagination.

From God we received our being, and it is his breath that keeps
life in us, that gives us our every smallest movement and thought.
Were he to leave us we should not be. From God, in Christ, we
received our other life—not as though we had first loved him, but
because he first loved us. And from him, in Christ, we daily, hourly,
receive that life of grace that keeps us alive as his sons. If we abide
in the vine we live and bear fruit. Left to ourselves we wither and
die. Every smallest act of virtue, in will and in deed, must come
from him—every good thought, every good desire, every good
deed. How then can we glory as if we had not received?

Humility is simply the practical recognition of all this. It is not
to be identified with self-depreciation. It is not a matter of preferring
others to oneself. It is, in the words of Bishop Ullathorne: " the

just and truthful expression in our thought, sense and conduct, of our nature, our position and our dependence as the subjects of God. It is the order arising out of that dependence."

CHAPTER II

THE FUNDAMENTAL VIRTUE

IT is almost impossible to find a book dealing with the spiritual life which does not stress the necessity for humility. We are told that without humility we are without any virtue, that unless we have humility we have nothing. The saints themselves continually aver the same fact. In face of such repeated testimony, we will hardly remain unconvinced. It is impossible not to agree that humility is important.

The same teaching meets us in the Scriptures. We are told that God resists the proud and gives grace to the humble, that humble prayer pierces the clouds, that the humble soul shall be saved. The Pharisees, the very personification of pride and self-sufficiency, are the only ones with whom Our Lord is intransigent. All others find forgiveness—Magdalen, the Good Thief, the woman taken in adultery, the Publican in the parable. But the Pharisees are whited sepulchres, full of rotteness and dead men's bones.

We cannot then believe that humility is something optional in the spiritual life. We cannot ignore these assertions and claim that we can get along quite well without humility, that it is something which will look after itself. We must be convinced that it is of great importance, and that it must be taken seriously.

Yet we may remain unconvinced of something else. Perhaps we are willing to grant the importance of humility, but we are not at all certain that it is of first importance, that it is the most important of all the virtues. After all, Scripture has hard things to say of other vices besides pride. Others as well as the proud are excluded from the Kingdom of Heaven. The scandal-giver for instance is told it were better he were cast into the depths of the sea. It is true that some of the masters of the spiritual life do speak of humility as the most important virtue, as the foundation of all the others. But it is easy to do that with quite a number of the virtues, and we may suspect that the most important virtue is the one the preacher or writer happens to be dealing with right now.

Thus we can say that charity is the most important, since all the actions of our lives deal with God or our neighbour. Or we can say that purity of intention is the most important. Hence it may fairly be asked whether or not it is true that humility is *the* most important virtue, in the absolute meaning of that phrase. If it is, then its necessity and the attention we should give it become obvious at once, but if it is not, then we cannot claim that it deserves more attention than any other virtue.

We may consider a virtue as important in two ways, either in itself or as preparing the soul for union with God. In itself, charity is the greatest of the virtues. The reason for this is that the virtues of faith, hope and charity are concerned immediately and directly with God, and the greatest of these is charity. Charity immediately unites us with God, and so is the first among the virtues.

But the main obstacle in us to the acquisition and growth of charity is pride. The perfection of the spiritual life consists in the perfection of charity—that is, that we love God more than all else, even more than ourselves. Pride, which is simply the excessive love of self, is completely opposed to this. Hence we can be certain that if we get rid of pride, charity will grow unimpeded. On the other hand, if pride is left unchecked, there will be little hope for any real development of charity. One of these must be supreme in the soul. You either love yourself more than God or you love God more than yourself. The two loves will not be equal. Either one or the other must be greater.

Now there are only two things that can hinder the growth of charity. It can either be choked by an excessive care for the things of this world, or it can be kept out of the soul by selfishness. If we eliminate these obstacles then charity will grow without hindrance, since we are naturally drawn to love the good, especially the Supreme Good, as known by faith. The practice of humility effectively attacks these two factors which keep us back from God. More than that, it removes them both simultaneously.

It ousts self-love, and at the same time removes excessive care for things other than God. If we constantly try to look at ourselves and all things else in the presence of God, we will not be deceived by the appearance of any creature. The direct effect of humility is a realisation of the nothingness of all things, ourselves included, outside of God.

That is why some of the saints have defined humility as the contempt of self. They do not mean to imply that the virtue consists simply and solely in despising ourselves for no apparent reason, much less in ignoring or denying our qualities. They mean that if we see ourselves in comparison with God the only good, we see ourselves as nothing, as despicable, as no-good. You either love God unto the contempt of self, or love self unto the contempt of God. In other words you must either be humble and have charity or be proud and be without charity. It is evident too that if we are in right relation to God, we will be so to creatures. If we love God more than ourselves, we will not use creatures selfishly. We will not allow them to occupy our hearts and lives to the exclusion of God and his love. Thus humility will establish us in charity.

If we compare charity to the bricks and mortar of which the spiritual edifice is built, then the function of humility will be the laying of the foundation. It removes the obstacles to charity. We must level the ground before the house can be built. In so far as it is the necessary preparation for the growth of charity, humility is the most important virtue.

But there is something else. One of the qualities of pride is its subtlety. It can be present in very many of our actions, and can act as a motive in much that we do, without our realising it. Humility is a testing virtue. If in time of trial or humiliation we remain steadfast in the practice of virtue, all is well with us. But who has not broken down sometime or other under trial? Which of us, if we have been honest with ourselves, has not been surprised at the strength of a self-love which had lain dormant for long periods until roused by contradiction? It is easy to serve God in time of prosperity. It is easy too to imagine that we are holy, when in fact we are simply spiritually asleep and free from temptation.

But let difficulties arise and how often have things appeared differently! At the time perhaps we did not see the affair in its true light. But afterwards, when grace and the love of God had reasserted themselves, did we not have to admit ruefully that there was little real virtue in our reaction? Who has not been at least tempted to say that he deserved better than this, that one could hardly be expected to take that sort of thing lying down, that after all a man has his rights, that we had worked hard and had a right to have our work recognised, and so much else besides? But how far is all that removed from true holiness! How unlike the reactions of the saints! How different was the reply of St. John of the Cross when, on his leaving for the Chapter of 1591, someone suggested that he might be elected Provincial: " I will be thrown into a corner like an old rag." How far are we from sanctity!

And why? Is it not because we are so far from real humility? Because in so much we do, even in our practice of virtue, we are seeking ourselves rather than the will of God. If in all we did we were detached and free from self-seeking, we would not be so resentful in time of trial. Because we want to do things our own way, and for our own sake, we become attached to them and seek results.

We can do this even in the practice of virtue, wanting the satisfaction of seeing ourselves become holy, rather than trying to do the will of God. What else is this but self-love—wanting to do things our way, wanting to order our lives ourselves, wanting to become holy in circumstances of our own designing? Is not all that a great pride, a setting up of self as the object of our actions, and a refusal to give to God his inalienable rights over us? Yet, who has never offended so?

St. Bernard says that without humility the whole edifice of the virtues is but a ruin. The metaphor is a striking one. What could be more pathetic than to see a man living in a ruined house? Would we not pity such a one—the windows broken, the roof holed and leaking, the walls crumbling, the door half-unhinged, the floor-boards rotting, the corners and recesses full of rubbish?

Yet there is something worse—to see a man not only living in a ruin, but happily convinced that his ruin is a fine dwelling-place with everything about it in order and good repair. Such a one, you would think, would truly deserve sympathy for he would be living in an unreal world of his own creation, out of touch with reality and truth. But the man without humility is such a one— he is living in a ruin which he believes to be a fine dwelling-house. He is unaware that the walls are cracked and tottering; until one day the wind blows and the rain falls and down they come on top of him. He is left naked in his pride and selfishness; he will be blessed indeed if he can see that the fault was his own, and begin to build again.

If the rot has gone too far, he may blame his neighbour, his superiors, his temperament which he cannot help, ill-fortune which dogs his steps, the fact that the breaks were always against him (which is a subtle way of blaming God's providence)—in fact everyone and everything rather than himself. But he will not build again. Rather than admit that he was wrong he will live without a roof over his head, kept warm by the sun of his self-esteem, which he mistakes for the light of God's grace, which dries up his heart and life, until in the end he becomes that withered branch which is of no use to the vine.

Humility then is fundamental, not only because it is the necessary preparation for charity, but also because it is the unifying principle of all the other virtues. To quote St. Bernard once more: " Humility receives, fosters and perfects all the other virtues." It is the unifying principle binding them together, the mould which shapes them. It is the fundamental virtue.

CHAPTER III

REVERENCE FOR GOD

Humility, we saw, consists essentially in an attitude of adoration in the presence of God, resulting from a correct understanding of our true place in his creation, and a realisation of our nothingness. This view of the virtue may perhaps be new to us. Many books dealing with humility stress the self-effacing aspect of the virtue to the exclusion of all else. This is correct, as far as it goes. But it does not go far enough. It is the truth, but it is not the whole truth.

Humility can be regarded from either of two view-points. One sees it simply as one virtue among so many, as part of the virtue of temperance. A virtue which must be exercised periodically, to suppress the uprisings of pride, in much the same way as any other virtue is practised at time of temptation against it.

The other view-point regards humility as an all-pervading attitude of soul, a habitual disposition of mind and will, which at all times looks upon God as infinitely adorable, and in doing so loses sight of everything else. It is in this latter sense—or rather in a combination of both senses—that humility is of such great and primary importance in the spiritual life.

Does humility consist essentially in preferring others to oneself? St. Thomas answers the question. Humility, he says, as a special virtue principally has regard to the subjection of man to God, on account of whom he also subjects himself to other men. It is true, he says again, that humility has the function of restraining the soul from tending inordinately to great things, but its root and principle lies in reverence for God. There it is—reverence for God. The exercise of humility will keep us in that place which is our due with respect to both God and our fellow men, but its source and fountain-head must be this sense of reverence. Without it humility cannot exist. With it the soul will be truly humble.

To say, however, that reverence for God must form the atmosphere of our life is not at all to say that we must adore God as Creator and Lord and ignore the fact that he is our Father and that he loves us. To do this would be to live in but half the truth. But the very function of humility is to place us in our true relation with God, and with each other. Contemplation of God should lead not only to love, but also to reverence.

It seems well to insist on this at some length. Reverence for God in humility must be the basis of our spiritual life. We must therefore understand this reverence aright at the beginning. Otherwise the practice of humility will inevitably appear less attractive. Insistence on the need of reverence for God seems to some a sort of recall to the spirituality of the Old Testament. We seem to be ignoring the love of Christ and going back to the lightnings of Mount Sinai to find inspiration for our spiritual life. In fact nothing could be further from the truth. But some of us have a more or less sentimental devotion to Our Lord, which for one reason or another we apparently find sufficient. Who has not met souls whose devotion to Christ is naturalistic and sentimental to a degree? It is true that they live devoutly and would suffer greatly rather than offend God; yet it can hardly be questioned that there is something confined, something narrow in their spiritual vision. Their love of Our Lord is mainly a matter of prayers and devotions, not of carrying the cross in desolation, in loneliness and in pain. It could be said that they hardly see the full splendours and riches of the Christian life at all—their spiritual horizon is the top edge of a devotional manual.

It may well be that such souls have never had the possibilities of that life pointed out to them. That they are lacking in breadth of view, or spiritual maturity, or liberty of spirit, because they do not know any better. It is beyond question that these souls will find a liberation, an undreamed-of breadth of vista in the full practice of a spiritual life based on that humility which is reverence for God. Because a devotion to Our Lord which does not include this is, at best, only half true. And no one can live at full strength on a half diet. The authentic mark of Christian sanctity is to be found in the story of the Magi: " And entering the house they found the Child and his Mother, and falling down they adored him." No stopping short at the delight of finding Our Lord, no resting content with the charms of the Divine Child, but the immediate recognition in him of the Great King—and falling down they adored him.

We used the phrase " a return to Mount Sinai," and suggested that it might occur to some as a description of humility. Such an idea would betray a great confusion of thought. But it is not easy to free oneself from it entirely, and perhaps we are more subject to it than we realise. Possibly we speak too readily of the Old Law as the law of fear, as though the Jews knew nothing of the love of God. Yet many of the instances that are usually adduced to show the awfulness of God in the Old Testament, can be paralleled by another incident showing the divine concern for man, the divine tenderness, the divine pity. God cast Adam out of the Garden, but he immediately promised a Redeemer. God came down on Sinai in lightnings and smoke, yet he allowed Moses to speak to him as to his friend. And we will seek long before we find anything comparable in tenderness and love to the Canticle or the pages of the prophet Osee. As God is depicted in this latter, indeed, he is the very personification of love.

This, however, is not the point we would underline here. The Old Law was the law of fear, as contrasted with the New which is the grace of Christ. St. Paul tells us that God was in Christ, reconciling the world to himself. God—the God of creation, the

God of Abraham, Isaac and Jacob, the God of the lightnings of Sinai, the God of the vision of Isaias and of the mysterious vision of Ezechiel—was in Christ. Christ is the great revelation of God to man, and let us not empty this revelation of any of its fullness.

Perhaps because we separate (instead of simply distinguishing between) the persons of the Trinity, perhaps because of the nearness and palpability of Our Lord, perhaps because of the sense of intimacy that Holy Communion brings, and because the Father seems to remain ever distant and mysterious, we find it difficult not to regard Our Lord and the God of Mount Sinai as different. We know, of course, that they are one and the same God. But in practice we find it just a little bit difficult to be convinced of that.

But Christ came to reveal God—that God—to us, so that knowing God visibly we might thus be brought to a love of the invisible God, as the Preface of the Nativity puts it. To know Christ, to come to the supereminent knowledge of him of which the Apostle speaks, is certainly not to minimise his divinity in any way. To love him perfectly does not mean that we shall meet him with a carefree attitude born of a wrong sense of equality which would bring him down to our level rather than raise us to his. Grace truly makes us sons of God, but what sort of son will not revere his father? Christ came to reveal God's love to us in all its fullness, but surely not that we might revere him the less. Hence if the idea of reverence for God appears to us to savour of the law of fear rather than of the new law, it would be well for us to examine our understanding of Christ and see if it is not perhaps lacking in something.

The Church, the bride of Christ, never makes this mistake of failing in reverence. To take but one instance. On Good Friday, at the unveiling of the Cross, we recall the great testimony of the love of God. Greater love than this no man has. Henceforth his love can never be doubted; it has gone to such a length, even to the death of the Cross. Confronted with this, recalling this supreme manifestation of the love of God in Christ, what does the Church do? She falls down and adores. She can, if we might so put it, think of nothing else to say or do than to repeat in awe-struck tones the Agios: " O Holy God, O Strong God, O Immortal God." There are few more inspiring moments in the Liturgy than this— and nowhere will we get a truer picture of what should be our reaction to the love of God. That God, the uncreated, self-sufficient

Other, should love me to the extent of dying for me in Christ. The sense of awe and reverence is heightened here in the actual discharge of the liturgy by the use of the unfamiliar Greek—as though our everyday words were insufficient to meet such a situation.

The profound reverence of the Good Friday liturgy here contrasts sharply with the attitudes towards Our Lord that are inculcated by some modern devotion. Having lost sight of the liturgy it substitutes sentimental formulae, that are not far removed from mawkishness, for the noble simplicity of the Church's prayers. In place of beauty we are given prettiness; in place of the stern realities of love, sentimentality; and in place of the sense of awe before mystery, a state of mind that would find the simple directness of some liturgical texts embarrassing and impolite. The liturgy has about it a purity of thought, a sense of appreciation of mystery, a reverence for everything divine, that are the accompaniments of enlightened love. But the little books of devotion too often substitute for these a lacrymose appeal to the imagination that is naturalistic and effeminate. It is the counterpart, in our devotional life, of repository art. Its cloying sweetness makes the reverence of the liturgy seem so strange that we mistake it for fear.

This reverence for God is shown us as the mark of the true Christian, not only in the liturgy, but also in the lives of the saints. St. Benedict puts at the very beginning of his ascetic teaching that we should always have before our eyes the fear of God, never forgetting what God has commanded and promised us; and remembering always that in all we do he sees us. What the saint intends the result of this teaching to be is evident when later he tells us that we should even handle the tools of the monastery reverently because they belong to God's house, just as do the sacred vessels.

There is little need to multiply examples, because it must be so. Sanctity must combine love and reverence, familiarity and holy fear. For sanctity is a coming to fullness of union with God in knowledge and in love, and how could increasing knowledge take from the reverence that should accompany love? None of the saints could ever forget their place before God. Seeing God for what he is, they did not take themselves to be more than they were. They saw themselves as nothing, and so they thought nothing of themselves. Why? Because they saw themselves in the presence of God, and in his presence they were as nothing. So they despised

themselves, they preferred others to themselves, they were glad
if others saw them as they saw themselves—but the root and
principle of it all was reverence for God. For humility principally
has regard to the subjection of man to God, on account of whom
he also subjects himself to other men.

CHAPTER IV

HUMILITY AND THE FEAR OF GOD

In the preceding chapter we were concerned to show that
insistence on the need of reverence for God is not a recall to the
law of fear. Reverence for God is a mark of the Christian spirit.
It is, however, by fear that God is revered.[1] Therefore it is clear
that fear of God has a place in the spiritual life. What is this place?

Does not St. John say that perfect love casts out fear? And yet
St. Thomas tells us that fear is the basis of reverence. It will be
useful to examine the question briefly here, and see if we can get
some definite principles on it. If fear is of use only at the beginning
of the spiritual life as St. John seems to imply, are we not delaying
the full development of charity by making so much of it in this
matter of reverence? The answer to these questions will show
further how mistaken we would be in identifying fear of God with
a servility that would inhibit love.

Before discussing the place of fear in the spiritual life, it will
be well to say something about its nature. Actually, a good deal
of the difficulty we find in reconciling love with fear would disappear
if we understood fear aright. In ordinary speech we use the word
" fear " to denote several things. It can mean a passion which is
instinctive and controlled only with difficulty. Or it can denote
the rational appreciation of a particular situation.

Fear as a passion or emotion is the same thing as being afraid,

[1] St. Thomas II-II q. 161; a. 2; ad 3.

being scared of something. When we feel this kind of fear, we grow pale, we perspire, our heart beats faster, and if it is bad enough we shiver. Now this has no place in the spiritual life. We are not meant to be afraid of God, or to be scared of him. His presence should not make us shiver with fright. Fear of this kind is always accompanied by a strong desire to get away from its cause.

In the second sense, fear is something rational, and could be called the apprehension of incurring the anger of someone. But here again we must distinguish. A slave will fear his master, who has the power of life and death over him, and who, we may take it for the sake of illustration, is tyrannical and capricious in his dealings with him. The slave in this case will be afraid of his master. Should we be afraid of God in this sense? No. It can be granted that the pagan idea of God was such as to give rise to this sort of fear. But St. Paul tells us that we have not received this spirit (of slavery in fear) but that of sons who regard God as their father.

Does a child fear its father? Yes, but in a manner different from the slave. The fear of the child is essentially a solicitude to avoid displeasing the father, and it springs from love. This is the fear the Christian has for God, and no matter how perfect love becomes it never " casts out " this fear. In the end the problem is essentially the same as that which demands that our idea of God combine his love and his justice. Neither rules out the other, and neither detracts from the other. Love and fear also combine in our attitude to God in that our love must be tempered by fear.

Our Lord himself tells us to fear God who can cast us into hell. At the beginning of the spiritual life especially, this fear will predominate and will play a more or less considerable part in our practice of virtue. We will avoid evil and do good because, in great measure, we fear the just anger of God if we do otherwise. " The fear of the Lord drives out sin," says the Wise Man. Such fear does not exclude love, otherwise it would not be good. It includes love, but of the two, fear tends to predominate. Hell, eternal punishment for sin, the possibility or even likelihood of incurring the anger of God, are always before us. The reason is simple. At the beginning of a man's conversion he usually needs a very strong force to turn him from the pleasures of this world. These have such a hold over most of us that the thought of God's love alone is not in itself sufficient to effect a radical turning away from them. Fear of the pains of hell is much more likely to do so. Hence the use God makes of that fear.

This is only the beginning. " Blessed is the man to whom it is given to have the fear of God," says Ecclesiasticus, " for the fear of God is the beginning of love." Gradually, as the soul progresses in the service of God, charity begins to predominate, and the influence of fear to lessen accordingly. The change will be only gradual, but it will be very real. We no longer have to recall the possibility of being punished by God in order to inspire ourselves to the practice of virtue. Love will become the mainspring of our actions. Fear will not entirely disappear, but it will no longer be the motive-force of virtue, " so that what we formerly did with difficulty, we will now perform without any labour and as it were by habit, not from the fear of hell, but from the love of Christ," as St. Benedict puts it.

Dom Marmion points out that we should never entirely lay aside such fear of God. It will be a useful weapon in the spiritual struggle if, as can happen, the strength of love seems in danger of being overcome by passion. But it will no longer be the main-spring of our actions. Its importance as such will diminish as we advance, and it will gradually give place to a new kind of fear. This is what is called reverential or filial fear. It is the fear of a child for its father, a fear which is an integral part of love. It is concerned rather with the possibility of being separated from God, and of not measuring up to his love, than with his punishments, and it will grow with charity, never disappearing from our lives.

St. John tells us that " perfect charity casts out fear, for fear has pain." He is speaking of that servile or initial fear that we dis-cussed above, the fear of God's anger and punishment. This is immediately clear if we understand the Evangelist's statement aright. The usual translation, which we have just given, is less than clear. The pain referred to is, in fact, punishment, and it is not a part of fear, but its object. Therefore the fear the Apostle is speaking of is simply that fear which has punishment as its object, and of course, perfect love casts this out, in so far as it transcends it. Understood aright the phrase needs no explanation. Modern translations render it, " Fear implies punishment or looks to correction," or by some such phrase. In so far as fear looks mainly to punishment it has no place in perfect love.

But with the casting out of this kind of fear will come growth

in the other—fear of separation from so great a good. For a man
who has a great love of God in his heart can never forget that God
it was who gave him that love. He can never lose sight of the fact
that he is of himself capable only of sin, and that if left to himself
he would effectively separate himself from God, who is now
everything to him. The virtue of hope gives us a certainty of
possessing God; but lest we be foolishly led to presumption, fear
complements hope, by reminding us of the possibility of losing God.
For that certainty of possessing him comes altogether from himself.
Fear reminds us that while God is anxious and ready to give
himself, we are, of ourselves, selfish and blind enough to refuse
the gift. The function of fear is to complement hope, by ensuring
that we not only fully trust God, but just as fully distrust ourselves.

So it was that during her last illness, when she was far advanced
in union with God and living all the time under the influence of
the Holy Ghost, St. Thérèse could say: " If I were unfaithful,
if I were guilty even of the smallest infidelity, I feel that over-
whelming troubles would come upon me, and I could no longer
face death." She went on to explain: " I refer to the infidelity
of pride. Were I to say, for example, I have acquired and can practise
such and such a virtue—immediately, I feel I would be beset by
the greatest temptations and I would fall." We are here faced again
with the double element in Christian perfection—the mixture of
hope and fear, of perfect confidence in God and complete distrust
of self. So far are these two from being incompatible that they must
necessarily go together, as each strengthens the growth of the other.

But this is not all. There comes a time in the life of the soul
when the Holy Ghost begins to play an ever more perceptible
part in its sanctification by his gifts. The gifts of the Holy Ghost
are " tendencies " placed in us by God, making us responsive to
the directions of his Spirit. The usual comparison between the
action of the soul in practising virtue and that of the Holy Ghost
acting on the gifts is that of a boat being propelled by means of
rowing or by the use of a sail. In practising virtue ourselves we
are like a man rowing a boat—the task is difficult and laborious,
and the rate of advance is slow. But if we hoist sail (by having
the gifts become operative)[2] we are carried along easily and speedily
by the wind, that is by the action of the Holy Ghost.

[2] We speak loosely here. This becoming operative does not at all depend on
us. but is due entirely to the Holy Ghost.

One of these gifts is fear, the fear of God. Its precise function is to complement the virtue of hope. It will, in fact, have been included in the fear we have already discussed, since the gifts are infused with grace and charity, and so are in the soul from the beginning. This fear, the fear of losing God, will remain a motive-power all our lives. We shall never outgrow it—rather the more we advance in charity, the greater will it also grow.

But its influence will be, not to frighten us, but rather to liberate us. It will liberate us from the great obstacle to union with God— love of oneself. How is this? By teaching us to distrust ourselves. Hope, we saw, assures us of the possibility of possessing God. Fear reminds us that we, of ourselves, are nothing but sin and selfishness, and that the only thing that can prevent our possessing God will come altogether from ourselves and not from God. Hence, distrusting ourselves, we shall find our all in God. In him shall we trust, evaluating all outside of him at its true worth, that is, nothing. Fear leads to humility, and humility is itself the oil that feeds the flame of fear.

It is evident now why St. Augustine identifies humility and poverty of spirit.[3] The perfection of humility is the complete getting rid of any trust in ourselves or in any creature—that perfect poverty which says not only that I have nothing but that I am nothing. But even if you take poverty in its literal meaning of the renouncing of material goods, it comes to exactly the same thing. Because the essential *mystique* of material evangelical poverty is that state of confidence in God and abandonment to his providence which looks for all from God. There is little gained by renouncing material goods if we do not look to the Father for all we need, and hope to receive all from him. Now the perfecting of that hope can be considered either as the work of humility, through Holy Fear, or the work of poverty, through a sense of the all-sufficiency of God. Because we know that in possessing nothing we possess all

[3] St. Augustine's commentary on the Sermon on the Mount:— " The poor in spirit are rightly understood here as the humble and those who fear God, that is those whose spirit is not puffed up. (Bk. 1; chap. 1). Blessedness starts with humility: 'Blessed are the poor in spirit,' that is those who are not puffed up, whose soul is submissive to divine authority, who stand in dread of punishment after this life . . . (Bk. 1; chap. 3). The fear of the Lord corresponds to the humble, about whom it is said: 'Blessed are the poor in spirit,' that is those who are not conceited or proud." (Bk. 1; chap. 4). The same ideas will be found in St. Bernard—1st Ser. for All Saints.

in that we will attain to the possession of God; we are glad to esteem all things as nothing, because God alone is all—which is where we started. " He hath filled the hungry with good things, but the rich he hath sent empty away."

CHAPTER V

THEIRS IS THE KINGDOM

T HE question of the relationship between humility and poverty was raised briefly in the last chapter. It merits a deeper investigation since it is at the very heart of Christ's teaching on humility. Any treatment of this virtue which ignores the Scriptural teaching on poverty of spirit will be shallow.

The text which is most often adduced in connection with Our Lord's recommendation of humility is: " Learn of me for (i.e. because) I am meek and humble of heart." In fact, however, Christ is not here telling us to learn humility of him, but is contrasting himself as a teacher with the Pharisees. These latter are proud and overbearing, but Christ is meek and humble. Therefore, that is, because of his virtue, his message commends itself to us. It can indeed be held that this is in itself a recommendation to us to imitate him. It is, but only indirectly. Our Lord is not directly concerned with teaching humility in this passage.

The most important text of the gospels on humility is the first beatitude: " Blessed are the poor, for theirs is the Kingdom of Heaven." Christ's use of the expression " the poor " here conveyed something very specific and definite to his hearers. The poor were a recognised group among the Jews. They were not merely those without material possessions, those without much of this world's goods. A man could be without possessions and not be poor.

The word poor as used by Our Lord here is practically a technical term denoting the God-fearing, the resigned, those who in trial remained faithful to God. Christ himself said at the beginning of his ministry that he had come to preach the gospel to the poor,

and he repeated this phrase when speaking to the disciples of John:
" The poor have the gospel preached to them." We might call
the poor here God's faithful ones. They were those who through
the long years of waiting and of trial had kept hope in him who
would come, who looked beyond this world for justification, who
did not put their confidence or trust in men or in themselves,
but in Jahwe.

In order to appreciate this concept of the poor and what it meant
as used by Our Lord, it is necessary to go back somewhat in the
history of Israel and see the development of the idea. Both St. Luke
and St. Matthew in speaking of Christ addressing the poor are
invoking the prophecy of Isaias, and in the synagogue Our Lord
applied the prophet's words to himself: " And he went into the
synagogue according to his custom on the sabbath-day. And he
rose up to read, and the book of Isaias the prophet was delivered
unto him. And as he unfolded the book, he found the place where
it was written: The spirit of the Lord is upon me, wherefore he
hath anointed me, to preach the gospel to the poor he hath sent
me . . ." [1]

It was apparently at the time of the Exile that the religious idea
of poverty really emerged. Before that the word " poor " already
had overtones of meaning beyond the ordinary connotation of
material poverty, but it was only during the sufferings of the Exile
that the idea took full shape. There comes into Jewish religious
thought at this time the idea that Jeremias is *the* poor man. Buffeted
by fate, stricken by God, attacked by his neighbour, he remains
the object of God's love, and remains faithful to him. From this
the idea gradually developed. The people themselves became the
" poor "—and in that they, and the prophet, were types of the
Messias who would be the great poor man. The text of Isaias just
referred to is, of course, post-exilic, and the idea finds further
development in many of the later Psalms.

It appears that God had as it were to impress this idea on the
proud Jewish soul by repeated trial and desolation. Faced with
their utter poverty in every sense—material and spiritual—the
people slowly awakened to the realisation that their poverty was,
in fact, their riches. To the poor the Messias would come, the poor
would Jahwe enrich, the poor alone would find salvation.

[1] St. Luke, 4; 16–18. The prophetic text is Isaias 61:1, *seq.* Note that Knox
translates it as " . . . to them that are humbled."

This is underlined in the texts of Isaias and the Evangelists we have considered—the poor will have the gospel preached to them. Not only did Christ come and do this, but in opening his Sermon on the Mount, he went out of his way to proclaim the poor blessed. The poor, those who have nothing, are promised the Kingdom. Even more, it is already theirs. They are the privileged ones. He had come to the poor, and for them he had hope and riches.

To be really poor is essentially to be dependent. The absence of goods and possessions is little. Of itself this is merely a material circumstance, a situation—but poverty is essentially a state of mind. Lack of property does not of itself induce dependence or detachment. But it can be a very powerful help and motive towards doing so, and that is why this state of mind is identified with poverty. If a man has no possessions in this world, then he has no security here, and his eyes and hopes should be on the world to come. As long as a man is secure in this world—is rich—then he thinks himself to have no need of God. " I am rich and made wealthy and have need of nothing. And he knows not that he is poor and wretched." [2] And as long as he does not know this he is not " poor " in the biblical sense. He does not await the expectation of Israel. The man who waits on God, the beggar by the road who cries out, " Jesus, Son of David, have mercy on me," is the poor man.

No one brings this out so well as St. Augustine in his Exposition of the Psalms. Take for example his comments on the 85th Psalm. This is one of the Psalms in which the poor man is the central figure and in which more than in most others he stresses his poverty.

> " Incline thine ear, O Lord, and hear me for I am needy and poor.
> Preserve my soul for I am holy.
> Save thy servant, O my God, that trusts in thee.
> I have called upon thee in the day of my trouble."

Now listen to St. Augustine: " The psalmist speaks in the form of a servant. For the Lord bows down his ear if thou dost not lift up thy neck. Unto the humble he draws near, from the proud he is afar off. To the rich then he bows not down his ear; but unto the poor and him that is in misery he bows it down, that is, unto the humble, and him that confesses, and him that is in need of

[2] Apocalypse 3:17.

mercy, not unto him that is full, who lifts himself up and boasts, as if he wanted nothing, like the Pharisees in the gospel. For the rich Pharisee boasted his merits, but the poor Publican confessed his sins.

" Those who are not proud are poor in God, and to the poor and needy and those in want he inclines his ear. For they know that their hope is not in gold and silver, nor in those things in which they seem to abound. Therefore when a man is one of those that despise in themselves everything that is wont to swell men with pride, then he is one of God's poor." The saint then refers to the fates of Lazarus and Dives, and asks: " Was it really for the merit of his poverty that the poor man was carried away by Angels, or was it for the sin of his riches that the rich man was sent away to be tormented? In the poor man is signified the honour which is paid to humility, in the rich man the condemnation which awaits pride . . . Learn therefore to be poor and needy whether you have anything in this world or not. For you may find a poor man proud and a rich man you may find confessing. The reason why one's prayer is heard is within—for I am poor and needy. Take care lest you be not poor . . . for if you are not you shall not be heard. Whatever there is around you or in you, on which you might presume, cast it from you; presume not in aught but God; be in need of him that you be filled in him. For whatever else you have without him, you are thereby the poorer."

It is unnecessary to comment on this. The poor man was the one who realised and felt his need of God and salvation, and whose attitude to God, therefore, was that of the beggar or the publican. Their poverty was not lack of wealth but humility of heart, poverty of spirit. Apart from Christ, this poverty of spirit reaches its greatest height in the Magnificat. Our Lady is the great poor one whom God filled and enriched beyond all understanding by giving her himself. And she is the perfect example of humility—realising her need, her own littleness, she realises too the goodness of God, who has given her all things, and so her canticle couples littleness and greatness, humility and exaltation, need and its fulfilment. But above all, she sings of the goodness of God.

We have said enough to bring out the fact that the poverty that Christ seeks in us, and which alone he promises to bless, is humility of heart . . . the realisation of our need. We are not concerned with tracing the history of the religious thought of Israel, but in showing something of the splendid riches that lie beneath the teaching of the gospels on poverty of spirit, and also beneath the virtue of humility rightly understood. It is a rich concept because it is a deep one, and the mere quoting of a gospel text does not necessarily reveal its depths. How the two virtues identify themselves in the practice of the spiritual life we have already shown. The essence of either is to realise that we are poor and blind and wretched, and to cry, " Jesus, Son of David, have mercy on me."

To the poor in spirit Our Lord promised the Kingdom of Heaven. What exactly is this reward? Perhaps an indication of it is to be found in the Apocalypse [3] where St. John describes the Kingdom, the New Jerusalem: " And death shall be no more, and God will wipe away all tears from their eyes." Who are the " they " referred to here? They are the elect of Israel, and earlier the Apostle had said of them: " They shall no more hunger and thirst, for the Lamb . . . shall rule over them and shall lead them to the fountain of the water of life."

We are dealing here with the perfection of the spiritual life—that the Lamb, Christ, should rule over us, and lead us to the waters of life. To be ruled in all things by Christ, to be completely docile to his ruling at all times, is to live altogether under the action of the Holy Ghost. This is holiness. And the fountain of life is life in the Spirit, which he himself promised to those who would believe in him: " If any man come to me, I will give him to drink." He had offered it earlier to the Samaritan woman—a water which would satisfy for ever those who would drink it. This then is the Kingdom—life in the Spirit, life drawn from the mystical spring flowing from the Heart of Christ. And the road that will lead us to this, to possession of the Kingdom and to fullness of life, is poverty of spirit, humility.

There is something further. The fruits of the Spirit corresponding to the beatitude of poverty are chastity and continence. Now St. John refers to virgins as those who follow the Lamb wheresoever he goes. Only virgins follow him everywhere. As though virginity were a requisite for both the invitation to follow him and the strength to do so. This again links up with what we have already said. Virginity, chastity, entitle and enable one to follow the Lamb everywhere—that is, to full possession of the Kingdom. But

[3] Cf. Apocalypse, chapters vii and xxiv.

virginity is the fruit of poverty of spirit, and possession of the Kingdom is the reward of it. Humility therefore, and it alone, will lead the soul through the purifying fires of continence, to the throne of the Lamb and possession of his kingdom. Not simply because pride leads to sin and because self-distrust is necessary for avoiding danger, but for a deeper reason. Because chastity is a fruit of the Spirit, borne on the stem of poverty, on the tree of humility, whose root is reverence for God.

CHAPTER VI

HUMILITY'S NEAREST NEIGHBOURS

In some of the following chapters it may appear that this or that act, which is listed as an act of humility, is really an act of another virtue. This may be correct. Sometimes we give as an act of humility something which is not humility but magnanimity. Again the virtue of meekness is often identified with humility, so that the two words are used interchangeably. This is not quite correct. For the benefit of those to whom these points may occur it will be well here to elucidate a few theological principles about them. Any extended discussion of humility will raise the question of the virtues which are so like it as to be identified with it in practice, so it will be well to see exactly where one begins and the other ends.

Let us recall here that the same act may be imperated [1] or motivated by several different virtues. For example, if a man is

---

[1] *Imperated:* This word, now obsolete in English, (cf. Webster) is retained here for the sake of precision. It is difficult to find a synomyn sufficiently exact. As used about a virtue, it is in contrast with "elicited." An act of a virtue is elicited if it proceeds directly from the virtue itself moved by the will. Thus an act of humility, done from a motive of humility is elicited by the virtue of the same name. But if the same act is done from a motive of, say, faith, it proceeds from the virtue of humility, under the impetus of the virtue of faith. It is said then to be imperated by faith. The following examples in the text make this clearer.

insulted by another, and he afterwards sees that other in need of help, he may help him from a motive of humility or of charity, or of both. If I meet with some trouble I may accept it from humility, considering that I do not deserve any better, or from a desire to do penance for my sins, or from love of God expressing itself in reparation, desiring to unite my sufferings with those of Christ in his passion. Or I may accept it from a mixture of all three. This is all the more to be remembered in that humility besides being one of the virtues, is also a general attitude of soul, springing from reverence for God and his order in creation.

That being so, it is still true that there are some virtues more intimately connected with humility than others. There will be faith, patience, religion and modesty as well as the more obvious magnanimity and meekness.

Faith will dispose us to humility. It will bring home to us the greatness of God and his rights over us, and consequently our own nothingness. Faith will keep us ever conscious of the fact that God has not only created us, but keeps us in being at every moment. It will remind us further that we are sinners, that we have abused the gifts of God so that only for his goodness we would be left utterly alone, " naked with our sins upon the barren earth." Christian humility is not some sort of natural virtue, but the humility of a redeemed sinner. Faith will supply us with all sorts of motives for humility, and will also motivate some of the acts which we ascribe to humility, such as reverence at Mass.

Much the same holds for the virtue of religion. Religion inclines us to worship God as we should. Its close connection with humility becomes evident immediately. Religion is, par excellence, the virtue which belongs to the creature as such. So also is humility. Therefore the religion of the humble man will be imperated by humility, and that explains what might appear to be an arbitrary ascribing of the effects of religion to humility. It also explains why some theologians consider humility to be part of justice.

The virtue of patience is also akin to, and closely linked with humility in practice. It is, however, of narrower scope, and its object is more closely defined. Patience consists essentially in suffering present evils in such a way as not to allow ourselves to be too much saddened by them. We are naturally saddened and depressed by any evil, that is anything that causes us to suffer. When we are depressed, we are less fit for work; and if the effect is sufficiently bad, we may be entirely unfit for anything at all. This tendency must be resisted, or sadness may so take possession of our heart that we are unable or unwilling to answer the calls of duty or of grace. This resistance is the work of patience.

The need for the virtue of patience hardly requires stressing. Daily, hourly almost, we need it, for so often do we meet with evils which tax us to support them. It may be illness—so slight as a toothache or so great as certain death from cancer. It may be a public calamity, or a very private one like a lost key. It may be a plain ordinary fit of the blues, one of our off-days, an uncongenial job, a difficult companion, a missed train. It may be any of a hundred things, big or small, which here and now are unwelcome and unwanted, and therefore constitute a present evil. To support them we need patience. Patience enables us, not merely to grin and bear it, but to carry the cross with joy, or at least with resignation. Without it, we fret and rebel and ask why did this happen to us. With it, we become a little like Simon of Cyrene.

Patience, then, is not identical with humility. It is concerned only with bearing present evil, while humility is rather a state of mind which is concerned with the whole of life and all the actions of a man. But evidently both virtues will come into play simultaneously. So if I find myself facing trials and difficulties of one kind or another, I will bear them patiently, from a motive of humility, not allowing myself to be too depressed by them, because I realise that I am only receiving what is my due. In practice it may well be very difficult to distinguish between the action of patience and that of humility. But then in practice we do not need to do so anyhow.

The other virtue we mentioned was modesty. We usually associate this with chastity, but it is of much wider application. Ecclesiasticus sums it up neatly: " A man's looks betray him. A man of good sense will make himself known to thee at first meeting —the clothes he wears, the smile on his lips, his gait, all make known the character of a man." Perhaps the best explanation of it can be had by referring to its opposite. There is an English word " impudence " which surely needs no explanation. If you consider its etymology you will see that it comes from Latin, and means in fact the opposite of modesty. Which is a rather roundabout way of explaining a very necessary virtue, but is none the less effective.

Once again, the connection, almost identity, between modesty and humility will be clear. A person will act modestly from a motive of humility, remaining silent, in the background, being self-effacing. It would be fair to say that the description of the humble monk given by St. Benedict in his twelfth degree of humility is essentially a description of a man who is modest from a motive of humility: " . . . that the monk, whether in the church, in the cloister, in the garden, on a journey, in the fields, or wherever he is, whether sitting, walking, or standing, should have his head bowed and his eyes fixed on the ground . . . " [2]

The virtue of magnanimity stands out among those immediately connected with humility. Magnanimity is the obverse of the coin of humility. It is the left arm to which humility is the right, it is the " give " while humility is the " take." Humility will enable us to resign a post; magnanimity will cause us to congratulate our successor. Magnanimity is a virtue which is rarely enough discussed or recommended to us, but without it our humility will limp. The very word itself is almost sufficient explanation of it—magnanimity —the quality of being great-souled.

We sometimes speak of a man being " big "—if he does something admirable, for instance, in the matter of forgiving injuries, receiving those who have offended him back into friendship, showing those who have opposed him in his plans or works that he trusts them and is ready to use their talents for the common good. There is nothing petty about him, we could not imagine him refusing to forgive an injury—he is too big for that. Or again he is in high office, but remains the most approachable of men. The job he is doing is evidently more important than himself. He can sit in council with the great ones of the earth, and yet remain simple and affable to all, and as " ordinary " as the least of us. You will hear it said of him that he has true greatness, for greatness never changes him.

What is this quality, what is this virtue he possesses? Magnanimity. We must not however, confuse it with a merely natural quality of leadership, or a natural dignity and superiority. The virtue of magnanimity is a real supernatural virtue, the supplement of humility. Christian magnanimity inclines a man to great things in the sphere of virtue. It is compatible with humility, which tends to make us keep the lowest place, in that it depends entirely on

[2] Rule chap. 7.

the power of God and his grace. It is the living realisation of St. Leo's famous phrase: " Christian, know thy dignity." We are of ourselves nothing, less than nothing, sinners—but we are the children of God, heirs of the promise, fellow-citizens with the saints. We can do nothing of ourselves, but our vocation is to the perfection of all sanctity and we know that the waters of life are ours for the taking. Nothing is beyond us—for we can do all things in Christ.

The magnanimous man is concerned with what is worthy of great honour. But the Christian sees that mundane and worldly things are in truth small and despicable, and so he strives for the " peak of true honour "—holiness and union with God. Seeing everything in true perspective he will not be elated by honours given him by others. Rather will he condemn and despise them, however great or small they may be. Likewise what appears dishonour to the natural man will not trouble his serenity, for he will be above it. Realising his dignity he will occupy himself only with what is worthy of him, that is the eternal. He will not allow himself to become occupied with trifles while life slips away and he hastens on unmindful of its real business.

So also he will not be dejected by slights, injuries, mistakes or injustice. His eyes are lifted up to the towers of the city that is to come. To be so small and mundane, so engrossed in the affairs of this world, as to allow his heart and mind to be occupied with such trivialities will be quite foreign to him. His face is towards the heights, he forgets the things that are behind and presses on to those that are before. Is he to sweep the kitchen? Is he to assist at a conclave? He will do either with the same zeal and devotion. For what matters is that they are both God's work and therefore both equally fitting for a Christian, both equally right and great in the true sense. " Christian, know thy dignity." [3]

The other virtue that is sometimes identified with humility is meekness. This again is quite a distinct virtue and of considerably narrower scope than humility. It is concerned precisely with the

---

[3] Those who are interested will find Q. 129, II–II of the *Summa* full of light on Magnanimity. The whole question should be read, Article 3 being especially noteworthy.

Aristotle (*Nich. Ethics*) is also worth reading on Magnanimity. His description of the magnanimous man makes very clear the difference between the Christian concept of virtue and the pagan one, and shows the necessity of humility and its distinctively Christian character.

keeping of our temper, its function being to restrain or moderate anger. In view of this, it is odd that meekness should be so often identified with weakness, and the meek man considered a feeble or spineless character. The opposite indeed is the truth, as is evident to anyone who has fought with the veritable demon of rising anger in himself. The control of anger demands very great self-mastery. Only the strong man is meek.

The weak character gives way to anger and is thereby led into all sorts of excesses. For nothing blinds a man so much and is so inclined to lead to precipitate action as anger. The author of the Ancrene Riwle, who wrote about six hundred years ago, lists the offspring of anger as seven: " contention, strife, vilifying reproach, cursing, striking, desire for harm of another, and the seventh is doing evil out of anger, or omitting to do good, or refusing to eat and drink or taking one's revenge in tears, if one cannot take it any other way, shouting one's head off in angry cursing, or in other ways doing harm to oneself in body and soul." An expressive description of the results of that weakness which is an uncontrolled temper, with its revenge, its grudges, its sulking, its nursing of resentment. And neither human nature nor bad temper has changed much since the time it was written. It is to the root of the tree that bears these fruits that meekness lays the axe. But again, its act may be imperated by humility.

Finally, for the sake of completeness, let us note the second beatitude—Blessed are the meek. The meekness in question here is not what we have just discussed, the virtue which controls anger. It is in fact almost identical with the poverty of the first beatitude. The meek are those afflicted by God, and resigned to their sufferings. But in this case the resignation is the principal feature stressed.

We could perhaps extend this list of virtues, but those given here seem to be the ones most closely connected with humility. If it happens that we meet an author apparently taking one for another let us not find fault with him. The fact is that, as St. Bernard puts it, humility receives, fosters and perfects all the virtues. We must not look for too fine distinctions—the essential is that we learn them by practice. Nevertheless a little precise knowledge of the connection between the virtues, especially those we are most concerned with here, may help to make the subject of our discussions clear.

CHAPTER VII

PRIDE AND VANITY

Lest we see sin where it is not, it will be useful here to give some account of the vices that are directly opposed to humility—pride and vanity. Pride is defined as the inordinate desire of our own excellence, while vanity (more exactly called vainglory) is an excessive desire for the esteem of others, because of our qualities, real or supposed.

Pride can be understood in either of two ways—as a sin in itself or as a sinful tendency, the result in us of original sin. As a special sin it will be rare, at least as a formal mortal sin. It was the sin of Lucifer and of Adam, but among men it will not occur frequently. Pride will be mortally sinful as such only in those cases where we deliberately seek our own good apart from God (that is, positively excluding him), or where we regard the goods we have as being strictly due to our own merits. Neither of these states of mind will be met with often.

The culmination of pride is the contempt of God, and this would be a truly satanic sin. But once again it will be very rare. What would be more frequent is contempt of God's representatives. This, too, could be mortally sinful, but the tendency which most of us have to criticise authority, would rarely go as far as contempt. It is not for that reason defensible, for more likely than not it does come from pride and preference of oneself.

While pride can be the cause of every sin, in fact many sins do not come from it, but from thoughtlessness, passion or ignorance. Left unchecked, pride can cause the greatest sins, even loss of faith. For evidently a certain humility is necessary to submit our judgement to that of authority. But in practice pride is not often the direct and immediate cause of loss of faith. There will probably have been a long and gradual process of erosion. A series of books, the talk of companions who themselves had no religion, the atmosphere of a godless society, have weakened the defences and prepared for the final collapse. Pride, or more correctly perhaps, vanity, could prevent one from confessing sins and so lead even to hell. But here again the personal factor can vary so much that it will be difficult to say there is mortal sin in any particular case.

These necessary reservations being made, it remains true that pride is the great obstacle to charity. In principle at least we are all so enamoured of ourselves that our love of God grows slowly and with difficulty. The wound of pride is the most difficult of all the soul's ills to heal. Its depths only come to light little by little as we try to eradicate it, and the devious twistings of our self-love are such as to defy analysis. Pride is the more difficult to see in ourselves in that it is a state and not an act.

St. Thomas teaches expressly that God sometimes allows a person to fall into shameful sins in order that his pride be cured.[1] Sins of the flesh are indeed less in themselves than formal sins of pride, but they are more shameful and so more humiliating. Since pride is essentially self-sufficiency, the only way in which his essential poverty and indigence can be brought home to the proud man is through the humiliation of seeing himself fall into such sins.

This applies primarily to the man who is so proud that he thinks he can do without God, but it would be a mistake to limit its application to him alone. Such a one is comparatively rare. More frequently to be met with, and therefore more practical, is the case of the self-righteous. The number of souls who allow their piety to breed self-righteousness is considerable. They are to be met with among all types of person, and no one can consider himself immune to the danger.

The temptation is the more dangerous in that it properly belongs to the devout. The sinner cannot consider himself better than other men, for he evidently is not. Hence the validity of St. Thomas's assertion about God curing pride by allowing sin.

There are few things more unyielding and impervious than the self-righteousness of the pious. They are generally quite blind to their own condition, but are ready to pass judgment on everyone else. Their very abhorrence of sin is less love of God than love of their own moral uprightness. It is not the idea of sin that shocks them, but the idea of anyone being so weak as to commit such sins.

[1] II-II; q. 162; a. 6; ad 3.

Their horror at the sins of others is really a pharisaical pleasure at the thought that they themselves are not as these adulterers and thieves. Their censoriousness is universal and they are convinced that it springs from charity. They can hardly be called smug, but their complacency is unshakeable. Despite their devotion and their prayers their soul is not so much encrusted with pride as plated with a veritable armour of it. Nothing can penetrate this except the humiliating vision of the squalid depths to which we are all capable of sinking.

How many there are who have served God for years, who are hard put to it to find sufficient matter for confession, and yet have within their souls this truly rock-hard pride! How often years of dedicated religious life, years of daily meditation, of sacraments received, of retreats made, have failed, not only to remove it, but even to make them aware of its existence.

Is this exaggerated? How then explain the self-justification, the refusal to follow advice, the readiness to blame others, the carping criticism, the fault-finding that are so widespread even among good people? They mean well, they say their prayers, but deep down within the idol of self stands upright and untouched. How the devil must rejoice to see the incapacity of such souls to advance truly in the ways of God! Did pharisaism die at the destruction of Jerusalem?

Never forget that in the parable the Pharisee is the good man— good, that is, by external standards. He is devout, he keeps the law, he fasts and gives alms. So he is pleased with himself and thinks that therefore God too must be pleased. He does not see that his good works, which are really good, are made sterile by the pride which inspires them and takes pleasure in them, that uses them to measure his sanctity and his degree of being better than his neighbour. In face of pride, even God seems to be helpless. So he allows sin, that its humiliation and shame may shake the scales from the eyes of pride, and in bringing the soul to its knees, bring it back to himself.

Pride is usually listed as one of the capital sins. Older writers, however, regarded vanity, which comes from pride, as the capital sin, and pride itself as something even greater than that. So St. Thomas and St. Gregory call pride " the queen and mother of all the vices."

Vanity differs from pride in that it seeks to be known to others.

Its sinfulness lies in wanting to be praised either for something we do not possess, or for something which is not praiseworthy, or by persons whose praise is not worth having. Everyone is tempted by vanity, and there is literally nothing about which one cannot be vain.

In order to strengthen one of his penitents in his struggle against vanity St. Ignatius told him that he himself had been beset by this temptation for years. For a long time after his conversion he was afraid to tell anyone what he had resolved to do for God, lest he would be vain about it. Similarly, on the night when he kept vigil before the altar of Our Lady in Montserrat, he was so afraid of vanity that he gave his clothes to a beggar in order to conceal his identity. And on the pilgrimage to Jerusalem he would tell no one of his destination lest he be tempted to boast of his doing the great pilgrimage. But St. Ignatius was not the first to feel this temptation. St. Paul himself, greatest of apostles, says that God gave him his " sting of the flesh," lest he be elated by the greatness of his revelations. So do not be too upset if you are tempted to vanity. At least you are in good company, and temptation does not mean that you may not yet be a great servant of God.

It is not sinful in itself to want to be praised, or to be glad when one is praised. Provided the reason for the praise is adequate, and the pleasure we take in it is proportionate and detached, all is well. It would be naïve, however, to think that such detachment is easily attained. There are few more heady wines than praise, and it is very difficult not to be pleased by it. No doubt a certain amount of this will be harmless and will rarely be more than a venial sin.

But vanity is a capital sin and therefore is extremely dangerous. It can lead to boasting, ambition, disobedience, resentment, hypocrisy, contention and a host of other evils, any of which may be a mortal sin. It can enter the soul of even the spiritual man so that he becomes vain because of his very spirituality. There is no essential difference between praise that is given for good looks or work well done, and that which is given for holiness and virtue. It is all praise of oneself, and any of it can lead to vanity.

Vanity is a remarkable vice in that it can glory in both holiness and sin. It can make us want to be called holy, and can lead us to boast of past sins. Men are more liable to this latter than women. There must be many a youth who was introduced to sin by taunts which his vanity could not abide. Many a man has got drunk, or worse, for the first time because his vanity urged him to be as " good " as those whose company he kept. And later on when the sins were forgiven and forgotten, vanity has recounted them, just to show that he too had " lived."

The vain man may boast of his family and of his wealth. Or of the fact that he has neither. " I am a plain man, educated myself, came up from nothing." He may glory in his learning or in his lack of it, in the books he has read or in those he has not. One may boast of his abstinence, another of his taste and fastidiousness in food. All he wants is that someone will tell him he is right in what he does, and is the more admirable for doing it. Not that he doubts this for a moment, but the voice of another saying so is sweet above all in his ears. He will talk of the good he has done or of the mistakes he has made . . . just so long as he can impress others, it matters not at all with what.

Vanity can seek glory in the externals of virtue as well as in the externals of worldliness. It can lead one to spend more time at the dressing table than at the prie-dieu, and to spend more money on cosmetics than on charity. It can make a religious prefer the poverty of an old habit and the singularity of a patched robe to the ordinariness of a good one. It can lead one to give too much attention to cleanliness, allowing it to degenerate into fastidiousness. Or it can have the very opposite effect—leading one to neglect oneself because of the glory that comes when others identify neglect with mortification, carelessness with detachment, and dirt with the desert fathers.

Vanity can lead a man to boast of his achievements, merely for the pleasure of hearing a passing word of praise. It matters not from where the praise comes, or that it adds nothing to the value of the work done. The better one is at any sphere of work, the more just does it appear that one should be praised. The sight of a person looking for praise and compliments is of all things the most despicable, yet vanity can blind one completely to such defects in oneself. It can lead to our asking advice when what we really want is to be told that we are right. We ask for criticism when it is the last thing we want; we suggest that our work is poor or faulty in order that someone will assure us that it is not.

Vanity is a vice that can enter secretly like a thief and almost take possession of our heart before we realise its presence. If left to grow unchecked, it vitiates all we do, reducing us to working

for that base motive—the praise of other men. Nothing is more
transitory or vain, nothing more worthless, nothing so liable to
change and alter without reason. Becoming dependent on it we
become dependent on the most fickle of masters, and sinning against
magnanimity we ourselves become small and mean.

The appetite of vanity grows in proportion as it is fed. The vain
man can never have enough praise, or enough recognition by others.
Impelled by vanity, he will work as he would never work even
for God. For glory has become his god and the maw of the idol
is a bottomless pit. If unable to gain glory from one thing he will
turn to another. Wealth or poverty, virtue or sin, souls converted
or scandal given, good looks or ugliness—there is nothing in which
he cannot glory, nothing on which he cannot feed his vanity.

The eradication of this vice is a slow and difficult business.
Good should never be left undone because of the danger of temptation to vanity. And it is better that what we do should not be
spoken of either, for the same reason. Whenever we do any good,
we may expect to hear the voice of the Tempter inviting us to
complacency, and sometimes the best way of being rid of him will
be to ignore him. But never give up the fight. And if you are tempted
to say, " It's only a venial sin," remember those men of whom
St. John tells us, who believed in Christ but would not acknowledge
him, for they sought the glory of men rather than the glory of
God. Even to such lengths can vanity go.

CHAPTER VIII

GRACE BUILDS ON NATURE

HUMILITY is misunderstood more often and more completely than any other virtue. Because it leads a man to give place
to others, to prefer others to himself and generally to deny himself,
it is frequently identified with some form of weakness of character.
We cannot imagine a truly humble man leading or directing others.
We cannot imagine him being a great teacher. We cannot see him
undertaking any great enterprise. This is unfortunate, since
inevitably it makes the humble man seem less a man for his
humility, and thus brings the virtue into discredit.

Not that we consciously discredit it. But we find it difficult not to be influenced by thinking of this kind, and in our hearts we may fear that humility is not a very virile virtue. Our study of magnanimity will have disabused us of this idea, at least to some extent. But the idea is not easily exorcised, and to some it does present a real difficulty. After all, grace builds on nature. Does it not therefore follow that if a man is naturally timid or even a trifle spineless, he is already half-way along the road to humility?

Timidity or self-diffidence is a natural defect. It may be anything from a slight bashfulness to a torturing fear of others, which is really a fear of oneself in the presence of others. Its effect may be so slight as to be negligible, or on the other hand it may completely paralyse your efforts at teaching or speaking in public. If timidity goes this far, so that it invades your efficiency in your job and makes you feel like a social outcast, it would more correctly be called a sense of inadequacy or inferiority. It is a common affliction, and deprives many of initiative and makes them shirk responsibility even though they are of good average talents.

Will such timidity help towards acquiring humility? No, definitely not. The practice of humility implies considerable strength, and its conviction of our nothingness has nothing to do with a natural sense of inferiority. Humility is primarily concerned with God, not with ourselves. It is based on God's greatness, not on our own feelings.

The one connecting feature between such timidity and the practice of virtue is that it may possibly inhibit temptations to ambition. A naturally timid character is unlikely to seek office or positions of responsibility. If these are offered him he will be likely to refuse them, or at least not be attached to them. But there is nothing virtuous about this. It is a merely accidental natural circumstance, and no more implies humility than a dislike of wine implies supernatural temperance. In the same way a naturally frigid character will not suffer from temptations of the flesh, but he will not for that be supernaturally more chaste than another who is greatly tempted. The timid are as fond of praise and are as ready to accept flattery as anyone else is. Which indicates that there is a great deal of difference between timidity and humility.

An inferiority complex has nothing to do with humility. Such a complex consists essentially in an unconscious flight from the repressed idea of one's inferiority. It is therefore involuntary, and is most likely due to some suffering in childhood, an over-strict education or the like. Since a complex will show itself in eccentric behaviour, such as over-aggressiveness, it will not even appear as pseudo-humility. It is an emotional sickness, and the sufferer from it needs psychiatric treatment, not an examination of conscience. We could perhaps call its manifestations pseudo-pride, but the similarity between its signs and those of true pride is only superficial.

Calm recognition of our inferiority should not be confused with the sense of inadequacy that we have mentioned. Such a recognition is the healthiest reaction to inferiority, and is desirable. It will entail facing our defect or lack, and either accepting it contentedly, or else using it as inspiration to develop some other trait that we do possess. Many famous men in all spheres of achievement have been motivated in this fashion, so that without the original lack they would not have achieved the success they did in some other field of activity. But again, all this is not humility. The recognition of our defects demands humility indeed, but it is not identical with it. Apart from any question of supernatural virtue such acceptance of ourselves as we are is a good thing, and will foster contentment and mental health. In the sphere of virtue it will be a question of accepting God's providential dispositions for us, and this demands humility. Humility could consist in accepting a neurosis, such as a strong sense of inferiority, and living with it. In this way the practice of humility will make for the development of the whole man, natural and supernatural. But it would be a mistake to think that such humility will obviate or cure mental illness. It will not do so any more than it will cure physical disease. Both need the care of a doctor, and abandonment to God's will is no prophylactic for either of them.

Some of these conditions can lead to diffidence or even self-criticism, which may superficially appear like an effect of humility. But at the heart of all such states is a neurotic inability to face reality. Whether this inability is conscious or otherwise makes no essential difference—in either case it is a flight from reality. Humility is a supernatural virtue, and consists in facing reality, the great reality of God and our place in relation to him.

Again the desire to avoid responsibility and the burdens of office can come from a variety of causes, none of them connected with humility. Prudence may lead us to decline a post. The belief that we will do more good elsewhere could have the same effect. So too could laziness. We may not want to be bothered with having to look after a school, a community, a group of young apostles. A man may be so settled in fixed habits that he does not want to be disturbed, preferring to have for his own exclusive use his periods of leisure, reading or study. This is selfishness and bears no relation to any virtue, although externally it may appear like humility. Our attitude should be that of St. Martin—I refuse not to labour— while at the same time not seeking or desiring office. To prefer one's own ease and comfort to all else is certainly not humility.

In all this matter of natural qualities or defects that appear to resemble humility, we must take care to distinguish between the natural and the supernatural. If we are naturally shy, quiet, retiring, we will give place to others easily and without effort. To a man of retiring disposition and studious habits, the idea of his being a superior may well be appalling. This is not virtue. To think that it is would be to risk going through life in a state of practical naturalism, without ever really practising virtue. A natural tendency to retirement and self-effacement is no more humility than a natural dislike of crowds is a contemplative desire for solitude.

These considerations should warn us about judging others. A man may be temperamentally quick to action, vivacious, eager. We should not conclude that therefore he is lacking in humility. If one is naturally gifted, one cannot help being aware of the fact, at least to some extent. If I am a successful lawyer, there is no point in my attributing every case I win to the leniency of the judge. If I am a good cook, that fact remains true whether I admit it or not. There is nothing gained by my asserting that I cannot boil an egg, whenever I am complimented on my cooking. Humility does not demand that a good mechanic declare that he does not know the difference between a spanner and a screw-driver, when his work is praised. That is not virtue; it is foolishness.

Because he knows his capabilities from past experience, a man may be coolly self-confident on being given a difficult assignment, and may declare his confidence in his work. Some persons are naturally like that, nothing dismays them, they are ready to undertake anything. It does not follow that they are wanting in humility. In fact they may be very humble indeed. They may realise fully that their talents and capabilities are God's gifts and that they owe everything to him. They may also be conscious that the possession of such talents brings with it the obligation of using them for the good of others, and not letting them lie fallow and unused. Humility does not demand this latter. Neither does it call for false self-depreciation, which indeed is not virtuous at all but the opposite. Humility does not consist in a low opinion of oneself or of one's capabilities. It is not an opinion of oneself at all. As long as you are trying to think badly of yourself, you are thinking of yourself. But humility is essentially a matter of forgetting yourself. It must not be judged on externals, in ourselves or in others. There is only one certain test of the virtue, and that is humiliation. The acceptance of humiliation alone shows the depth and reality of our humility.

There is one precious gift which is already a sort of natural humility, and that is a sense of humour. What is a sense of humour? It is not the ability to laugh loudly. Neither is it a capacity for an unending stream of wisecracks and repartee. Still less is it a frivolity of mind and outlook that pokes fun at everyone and everything.

A sense of humour is essentially a sense of perspective. It is an understanding that comes from a true sense of proportion. " Humour is not a matter of laughing at things, but of understanding them. At its highest it is part of the understanding of life " (Leacock). It is an ability to see ourselves as we really are, and to smile at the comic figure that the biggest of us cuts in strutting across life's stage. A sense of humour enables us to appreciate the littleness of all that passes, and the strangeness of the ordinary, especially of ourselves. Indeed we might say that a sense of humour is a specifically Christian thing, for only the Christian can see himself and all else in true proportion, since he sees himself and life against the backdrop of eternity.

The man with a sense of humour will be able to laugh at himself. He will see how unimportant he really is, and consequently how unimportant are his mighty words and works, his successes and failures. He will realise that he is not the only worker in the vineyard, and that the harvest does not depend on him alone. He will realise that neither he himself nor his work is so important that the failure of either will arrest the course of history.

A sense of humour will save us from self-importance—that

occupational hazard of all promotion. It will keep us from strutting instead of just walking, from taking offence at trivialities, from acting as though we had all the answers and no one else had any of them. In short, it will save us from taking ourselves too seriously and from thinking that everyone else should take us seriously too. Among the natural gifts a sense of humour is one of the greatest.

To conclude—humility is of all virtues the most virile and mature. It implies a capability to see ourselves as we really are, and of acting accordingly. The weak character, the immature, the self-conscious, much more the neurotic, has little in common with the humble man, however much the two may appear to act alike superficially.

CHAPTER IX

WE ARE UNPROFITABLE SERVANTS

IN view of what we have already said about reverence for God, we could define humility as a practical sense of the divine (Msgr. Gay). Whenever we meet with God or his action—whether in himself, in the events of our lives, in our neighbour, anywhere or in anyone at all—we humble ourselves, we bow down and adore. The essential act of humility is to render homage to God, to acknowledge our subjection to him and give him all glory. This means not only accepting God's will but also his providence. As this latter is the more frequent, it is perhaps the more important. Certainly it is the more difficult. But to do so, especially in deed, by the practical adoration of a loving act of our will, is the very essence of humility. It is essential to the practice of the virtue that whenever we meet with God or his action, we adore—however veiled or hidden the appearances, or however painful or contrary the action.

If we would find a single general formula covering this attitude in all its acts, it is that of Christ in the gospel—" Say we are unprofitable servants." If we succeeded in developing this outlook and attitude to life, we would be truly humble. For we would recognise everything that comes to us, whether pleasant or unpleasant, easy or difficult, satisfying or disagreeable, as being in fact better than we deserve. We would recognise that everything comes to us from the hand of God, and is therefore right and good, only we cannot always see it so.

There is an incident in the life of David which is worth recalling. Absalom had risen in revolt and David, his father, had been forced to flee Jerusalem. " And he came as far as Bahurim and behold there came out from thence a man named Semei, and coming out he cursed. And he threw stones at David and he said: Come out, come out, thou man of blood, thou man of Belial. The Lord hath repaid thee for the blood of the house of Saul. And one of the king's servants said: Why should this dead dog curse the king? I will go and cut off his head. But the king said: Let him alone and let him curse; for the Lord hath bid him curse David. And who is he that shall say: Why hath he done so? "

We have here in David and his servant, the contrast between grace and nature. The natural reaction is: Why should this be? That of grace is: The Lord hath bidden it. David was filled with that practical sense of the divine of which we have spoken. He was here overwhelmed with trials and difficulties. His own son had risen against him and had sought to destroy him. The people seemed to be abandoning him. Then came his enemy to curse him and pelt him with stones. His reaction was not: This is too much; I deserve better than this; this must not be allowed. No, he immediately sees the hand of God: The Lord hath bid him curse me and who shall dare to say, why. This last sentence is a splendid flaming one. David was not simply resigned, ready to accept God's will because he had no option. No, rather would he embrace it with all his soul, so that he would say to anyone who questioned it: Who will dare to say, why hath he done so?

Now what has this to with humility? Precisely this: this is humility. It is the very essence of the virtue. The attitude of mind and heart which is exemplified here in David, is humility. The essential act of humility is to give God the glory and render homage to him in all we do; it is principally concerned, says St. Thomas, with the subjection of man to God. What we must try to cultivate in ourselves is that attitude of dependence on God which not only makes us look to him for help, but especially makes us recognise everything as coming to us from him. We must realise that we depend on him. That we are continually, in all we do and in all that happens to us, in the shadow of his hand. Everything, without exception, comes to us from his providence. Therefore our attitude to him and all he sends can only be one of reverent love.

Further we must realise that he treats us infinitely better than we merit. We can never truly say: I deserve better than this. The fact is that we do not deserve life or love or grace at all. For when we have done all that is commanded us we must still recognise that we are unprofitable servants.

If only we never failed in this, how great perfection would be ours! For which of us has never said or thought: I deserve better than this. If we want to practice humility and come to its perfection it is especially by putting into action this principle given by Our Lord himself that we will do so. It is the teaching of the saints which Father Olier sums up admirably: " In sickness, in persecution, in contempt, and in any other affliction we must take God's part against ourselves and acknowledge that we justly deserve all that and more; that he has a perfect right to use every creature for our punishment; and that we must adore the great mercy he uses towards us, knowing well that according to his justice we could fare far worse."

There is no situation in which the " unprofitable servant " principle will not stand to us. Is it correction? We recognise God's mercy. Is it a false accusation? We remember our sins and are glad to suffer something for them. Is another preferred to us? We deserve no better. Are our talents and capabilities ignored? It is but as we deserve. Are we praised? Of ourselves we do not deserve it. Therefore there is no danger of our resting in it, or of seeking it.

Are we promoted to office? We know that we cannot do any good of ourselves, and we will come to the task with due humility. Thus there will be little danger that we will obscure the vision of God for others by putting ourselves in his place. Likewise, a fitting respect for those under us will never be wanting, and yet we will always remember that we represent God, and we will never allow others to overlook or forget this. Are we removed from office? No one is less surprised than ourselves. There is no repining, no envy of our successor, no blaming of our superiors or those over whom we had authority. No matter in what situation we find ourselves, the principle holds good and answers the question as to how we should act.

In time of trial especially we will find this " unprofitable-servant " principle of use and value. We said earlier that there is only one real test of humility, and that is our acceptance of humiliation. By this we mean those humiliations which are imposed on us from outside, not those we freely undertake ourselves. These latter have their own use, but we can so easily deceive ourselves with them. We are so selfish, and our ego is so averse to real humiliation and so adroit at escaping from it that there is great danger of feeding self-love in undertaking humiliations of our own choosing. We may be willing to tell ourselves, or even tell others, that we are the greatest of sinners. But let someone else accuse us of the merest peccadilloes and we soon see how humble we really are.

No! Infinitely safer and surer, if we accept them aright, are those providential visitations in our lives which humble us effectively—failure, mistakes, misjudgement, loss of reputation, being passed over, being ignored, perhaps even sin into which God may allow us to fall to show us what we are. In all these matters nature's response will be to assert that we are right, that we are misjudged, that the accusation is false, that we could not help it. To accept them as loving visitations of God—the Lord hath bid it, and who shall dare say why?—we need faith and humility. Faith to remind us that they come from God, however much he may use secondary causes, and humility to remind us that we deserve them and more.

Humility, and it alone, will answer to humiliation: We are unprofitable servants. To accept the fact that we have failed, despite our best efforts, that our work is brought to nothing by a misguided successor, that our motives in all we did are questioned, that those for whom we have worked have turned against us, that sickness or perhaps old age face us with years of apparent uselessness or inactivity—to accept all these without complaint demands great humility. Always to think that whatever comes to us is better than our just deserts, never to say that fate has been unkind, that Providence has dealt hardly with us, above all never to say that we deserved better—that is humility.

CHAPTER X

DEGREES OF HUMILITY

Iᴛ must not be thought from our treatment of it in the preceding chapter that humility is a merely passive virtue, whose only effect is to enable us to submit to the dispositions of Providence. No, but that is the sphere in which humility will most often be demanded of us. That also brings out better than most other illustrations the true nature of the virtue. It is too, as we shall see more fully later, the real testing-ground of humility. What we might call the active aspect of the virtue is summed up by the *Imitation of Christ* in the immortal saying: Love to be unknown and esteemed as nothing.

Does humility demand that we do this? The answer is apparent if we reflect on the meaning of the virtue. We see that we are sinners, that we deserve nothing of ourselves, that in justice we can never complain. Now it is an easy and a natural step from this to seeking the last place. If we are convinced of our unworthiness, then we are convinced that the last place belongs to us by right. So we will seek it—the place where we will be unknown and esteemed as nothing.

Before we discuss this question, we would draw attention to a very important fact. It is this. There are degrees of humility. This is a truism—yet it is often forgotten or ignored. And ignoring it leads to misunderstanding the virtue, and perhaps to finding its practice impossible, and so to discouragement. Why is this?

Many of the saints and spiritual masters, in teaching us how to acquire humility, go right to the heart of the matter by concentrating on this " last place " aspect of it. They tell us to seek the last place, and that if we do so we will be humble. This is not an attractive doctrine, and it is extremely mortifying. It is also, of course, very powerful if followed. But if not understood aright, its practice can lead to failure and so to discouragement. It could also indeed lead to eccentricity. Always to take the last place, always to prefer others to oneself—this is a hard saying. Of course it is. It is high holiness and not the work of beginners. And we must, in this as in everything else, begin at the beginning.

The saints called themselves the last of men, the greatest of sinners, and wished that others would treat them so. Now this is admirable, and perhaps one day we shall be able to imitate it. But it will be well to remind ourselves that we cannot do so yet. Not by a long way. If you do not spontaneously think yourself the greatest sinner in the world, then do not try to convince yourself that you must be. Forget about it. If you succeeded in doing so you would probably be proud of it, anyhow.

No! Remember the degrees and begin at the beginning. Walk before you run, much more before you fly. Have enough humility to realise that you have very little. Much better admit to ourselves that there is considerable room for improvement in our actions than to try and imitate the saints too closely. This latter may come in God's good time. In the meantime, let us admit that we are sadly lacking in humility and set about practising it in the small ordinary actions of every day. In this way we will not outstep grace, and risk making the practice of the virtue distasteful. The very realisation that we need to do this will itself be good exercise in humility.

We can try to be humble in our relations with others. To respect everyone we come in contact with, to realise that however the person we are dealing with may appear, he is in fact as good a man as ourselves, as we say. But the trouble is we do not believe it. We must try to acquire a humility that will enable us not to look down on anyone, not to consider ourselves superior to anyone. It is a long way from the humility of the saints to think less of anyone because he is uneducated, or poor, or down-at-heel. Much less will we criticise anyone for his apparent lack of virtue. " We are all frail, but see that thou consider no one more frail than thyself." If we can arrive at respecting everyone, we will have achieved a great deal.

So too if we can bring ourselves to rejoice in the gifts and accomplishments of others, not considering that their success entails a reflection on us or puts us beneath them. To be glad at seeing another exalted, in however small a way, to try to be glad too if someone has more talents than we have, and to avoid anything like criticism of him, or the more subtle condemning by faint praise. Never to let ourselves give way to that attitude towards another which makes us remark that he may be very accomplished, but it is a pity he does not do so and so, because we are unwilling to admit that he is superior to us, but rather to praise him in all sincerity.

Again if we are praised, it will not be necessary or desirable to proclaim that, far from deserving it, we are the least of men. This would be undesirable singularity. A small silent prayer for humility in all we do will be much better. Further, without drawing attention to ourselves by doing so ostentatiously, we can quietly and unobtrusively keep in the background. We can avoid putting ourselves forward, making something of ourselves. We must, however, be careful here. If, for example, there is a general discussion going on in a group of which we are a member, it will be as well to contribute whatever we have to say, in simplicity and charity. But we can do so humbly, and without giving the impression that ours must be the correct solution to the problem. A studied effort to remain silent at all times, to seek the background so completely and effectively as never to say anything, will be lacking in simplicity and will be too self-conscious. Humility is a complete forgetting of ourselves, not a self-conscious fear of ever opening our mouths. The person who is simple and guileless enough to join in whatever is being said, and say what he has to say without reflection or premeditation is probably nearer real humility than the one who persistently seeks the background all the time. The ideal is to forget yourself, not to withdraw into isolation. What we must avoid is a spirit of contention, a readiness to contradict, a wiser-than-thou attitude.

All this is only a beginning of virtue, but it will be very pleasing to God and is the necessary beginning of the journey to the heights. The effort to practise humility in the small things of which we have given examples, will prove very mortifying too, in that it will be more or less invisible to anyone except God and ourselves.

But if this is the beginning, we can fairly inquire as to what will be the end. Can we point to a consummation of the virtue, to a perfection of humility, towards which by the help of grace we might aspire? It seems that we can do so, and that this perfection is to be found in the formula of the *Imitation* that we have already referred to. Love to be unknown and esteemed as nothing.

There is in every man a desire, perhaps the deepest-rooted and most fundamental desire there is, to be " something." It must not be confused with ambition as that is usually understood.

Ambition is something much grosser, much less subtle. This other desire will remain even after we have effectively overcome ambition. It is the last bastion of the ego, the last ditch where the self, driven further and further back by the onward spread of grace throughout the soul and its activities, will make a desperate stand. It will not manifest itself as a desire for power, or for honour, but simply as a consideration that it is better for us, in view of the possible good we might do, to be well thought of. It is not that we seek a great reputation, but that if we are to have any influence on others, if we are to work at all effectively in spreading the Kingdom, we must be well thought of.

Now while this may be true, it may also be a subtle attack of the devil. This desire to be well thought of, to be esteemed as something, is the only temptation of Our Lord that was repeated during his life. Once he conquered the others in the desert they were over and done with. This one recurred twice. The first time when the disciples said: " Pass from hence and go into Judea that thy disciples also may see the works which thou dost . . . If thou do these things, manifest thyself to the world." It recurred again on Calvary, at the hour of Jesus's apparent failure: " If he is the king of Israel, let him come down from the cross and we will believe in him."

It was precisely by the failure of the cross that Our Lord achieved the purpose of his life here on earth. Is the disciple above his master? It is true that we must work for the spread of the Kingdom, but it is also true that we do not know precisely what service God wants of us. Hence, we must be very pliable and ready to obey the indications of his providence. Otherwise, by asserting ourselves we risk upsetting his work. It is for him to call us to action, to set us as a city on a hill. But it may well be that he will draw more good from our remaining hidden and little; and to refuse this will end any real working for him on our part. It is essential that the grain of wheat die before it can bear any fruit. It will demand humility thus to die. And it will be the perfection of humility to love this death; to love to be unknown and thought nothing of.

To choose this, to prefer this to anything else—that is great virtue and high perfection. Hence it is not something that we will attain in a day or a week. Rather will it entail a long and weary journey, much struggle and much failure and much patience. But it is the goal towards which we can aim. It is the very summit of humility—when we have uprooted the last remnants of a pride that above all else desires to be " something." To be something appears not only good but even necessary; to be well thought of for any reason, and the more spiritual the reason the less will it appear as pride. Anything rather than that crushing annihilating ignoring of us by others. " We esteemed him not."

St. Thérèse of Lisieux is a remarkable example of this. We remember how, when she lay dying, one of her religious sisters remarked that they would have nothing to say about her in the obituary notice. " She never did anything." God had cast her in the furrow of Carmel. She had done her part—she had died completely and effectively to herself. She left the fruit altogether to God. So too with us. What God wants is not great works and deeds but that we should come to him in the perfection of love. Precisely how we should bear witness to him is for him, not for us, to decide. Our task is to humble ourselves completely. For when the soul, says St. John of the Cross, shall have attained to complete annihilation, which is nothing else than the deepest humility, then will take place the union of the soul with God which is the highest state attainable in this life.[1]

CHAPTER XI

GATHER UP THE FRAGMENTS

In any lengthy discussion on humility a number of topics inevitably crop up, some of them posing genuine problems, that merit discussion. We shall use this chapter to tie up some of these loose ends.

There are, for instance, the questions of self-imposed acts of humiliation, of the desire of approbation, the possibility of truly believing oneself the least of men, one's possible reaction to the loss of one's good name. There is also the objection which is heard nowadays, that the practice of humility in the traditional manner is not suitable for us moderns, and that it leads to undesirable consequences. A brief treatment of these topics will not be out of

[1] The penetrating treatment of this question by Dr. Leen, C.S.Sp., in *Progress through Mental Prayer* (Chap. VIII) should be read.

place. While we cannot hope to answer all possible difficulties, we may succeed in meeting the main ones.

First, the desire of approbation. This in itself is not a bad thing. It is true that if it is excessive or if we allow ourselves to be carried away by it, it becomes evil and a sin of vanity. But in itself it appears to be merely a natural desire and not necessarily opposed to humility. Humility does not mean we must be ignorant of, or blind to the gifts God has given us. Neither does it consist merely in a lack of conceit. Nor does it lie in having others fail to see our gifts or talents. True humility goes much deeper than that. It should enable us to recognise to the full all the gifts God has given us, to thank him for them, and to realise how unworthy we are of them, and how poorly we use them. Ideally we should be able to have the gifts of God praised in us, without taking the praise to ourselves.

What is essential is that we use our gifts only according to God's will and never merely for self-glorification. Then if we are commended for something we have done, we can be glad in all simplicity and our humility will not suffer. And on the other hand if no one notices and no compliments come our way—well, we shall not be upset; we are unprofitable servants and do not deserve commendation in any case.

It will help too if we remember something else. There is nothing supernatural about it. Nine times out of ten when people pay you a compliment they are only making conversation, and the only sensible thing to do is to answer, " Thank you," and forget it. But admittedly there is the tenth time. The principle given above holds for it.

While on this subject we would make a further point. Superiors should not be too anxious about injuring the humility of their subjects by praising them. While taking care not to allow those under them to work merely for praise, it does not seem very wise to go to the other extreme and never praise them at all. An occasional word of commendation can be a valuable aid to self-respect and community spirit. No doubt, in theory we should be convinced of our own unimportance, of the fact that we are not indispensable. This should lead to humility. In fact however it more often leads to discouragement and loss of zest in work. The average person needs to feel wanted, if not needed. While he must be encouraged to work for God, and not for superiors or for praise, he does need to feel that his work is appreciated. Otherwise he is liable, unless he is a man of rather rare virtue, to develop a *laissez-faire*, " couldn't-care-less " attitude, which is inimical to spiritual progress. Abandonment to God's will is the ideal, but the dividing line between it and disinterest in work and responsibility is finely drawn. An occasional word of praise might save a person from this latter, without in any way injuring humility.

About imposing external practices of humility on ourselves we have already spoken. There is need for the greatest care here, and generally speaking it should not be done at all. Rather what we should aim at is a great fidelity to all the external practices of the virtue which belong to our state, as religious for instance. Such would be the fundamental one of obedience, and then the other small but important acts, contained in every religious rule. We can be content with what is poor in externals. If we have a choice, we can, without losing our liberty of spirit, prefer what is mean or laborious or little. Also we must take great care to avoid singularity or any drawing attention to ourselves or our qualities. Here again, however, prudence is needed. To resolve never to speak of oneself would not be advisable. This would be too self-conscious, and lacking in simplicity. Better simply try and avoid excess. So too we should never speak evil of ourselves. To do so requires very great virtue, and will do no good but possibly much harm if indulged in by the ordinary soul. At the very least, it will most likely lead to an increase of self-love.

We are talking here about speaking evil of oneself that is true. It is never permissible to tell lies about oneself, for any reason at all. One sin may not be committed in order that another be avoided. The attempt to avoid pride will not justify lies. Neither should one ever talk about one's own humility. This simply cannot be done except by a saint. " Professions of humility are the very cream, the very essence of pride. The really humble man wishes to be and not to appear so. Humility is so timorous that she starts at her shadow, so delicate that if she hears her name pronounced her very existence is threatened." (St. Francis de Sales). The one who is really humble has so forgotten himself that it never occurs to him to speak of himself at all.

St. Paul tells us " in humility to esteem others better than ourselves." This is absolutely necessary, for if we prefer ourselves to anyone then the love of our own excellence remains and humility ceases to grow. It is easy to esteem others better than ourselves if we compare what is bad in ourselves to what is good in them, or what is of nature in us with what is of grace in them. It may be objected that this is artificial and unreal. If I compare myself with another within the same terms of reference I must surely prefer myself, if I have greater gifts. That is so. Ideally we should be able to see all gifts, whether our own or others', as belonging to God, and so as something to be glad about objectively. However, the real answer to this problem is that it must be solved on one's knees, not out of a book. It is not, in fact, primarily an intellectual problem at all. Therefore any merely intellectual solution will be unsatisfactory. The real answer to it is to be found in the teaching of St. John of the Cross. Progress in this matter of preferring others to oneself only comes with advance in prayer, and this is what we should concentrate on, rather than intellectual comparison of ourselves with others.

In treating of the Night of the Senses the Mystical Doctor is explicit in teaching that one of its effects is the sweeping away of imperfections that belong to spiritual pride. " For," he says, " the soul sees itself so dry and miserable that the idea never occurs to it that it is better than others . . . it recognises that others are making more progress than itself. Hence there arises the love of its neighbour which it never forgets . . . it is aware only of its own wretchedness, which it never forgets, nor takes occasion to set its eyes on anyone else."

St. Bernard is worth quoting on the same subject: " Beware of comparing yourself either with those who are greater than you or with those who are less, with many or with one. For how do you know whether that very one, whom you perhaps regard as the vilest and most wretched of men, at whose life you shudder as being infamous and defiled with the greatest crimes; whom you think is therefore to be scorned, not only in comparison with yourself who are living, as you confidently believe, in temperance, justice and piety, but even in comparison with other criminals, as being of all the worst. How do you know, I say, whether he may not one day be made by the power of God to be better than you and those to whom you prefer him ? Or even whether he is not so now in the sight of God ? . . . So do not presume, I do not say to prefer yourself to anyone, but even to compare yourself to anyone." [1]

---

[1] Ser. 37 on the *Canticle of Canticles*.

As for considering yourself the greatest sinner, or the vilest of men, once again the intellectual solution is not completely satisfying. We can, we are told, reflect that if anyone, even a notorious sinner, had received the graces we have, he would have made better use of them. Therefore in a relative sense we are the greatest of sinners. That is true. But the humility of the saints in this question is something more than a mere intellectual conclusion. It is, in fact, an extraordinary grace. Theologians are of opinion that the self-abasements of the saints are the fruit of an altogether special light, infused by God, which gives such a keen appreciation of the sanctity of God and the beauty of sanctifying grace, that they see the smallest sin as hideous. This is a special grace given to the saints in order to keep them humble despite their exceptional divine favours and the veneration of the people.

What about the loss of our reputation? If our good name is attacked or destroyed, should we defend ourselves or should we suffer in silence? Well, first of all, we may have a duty to defend ourselves. Our reputation is one of our most precious possessions; it is necessary for social life. If one is a priest or a teacher, a superior or in charge of young people, one's good name is essential for the carrying out of one's work. Therefore we have a duty to our charges or subjects to clear ourselves if our good name is at stake. That is obvious.

But suppose one is just a private individual, with no such obligations to other persons. If we are accused of something grave we should clear ourselves if we can do so, likewise if we are accused of what would be a mortal sin. Otherwise scandal may be given, and harm will result. Even a hermit has a duty of edification— or at least of not disedifying or scandalising others. Where some of the saints, such as St. Gerard Majella, have acted otherwise, we must take it that they did so under the inspiration of special grace. Without a similar grace their conduct is not to be imitated.

Apart from that we should not be too anxious about our reputations. The ordinary faults of which we may be accused should not trouble us. If they do, it is probably due to wounded pride or vanity rather than zeal for truth. As the *Imitation* puts it: " It is good for us to suffer contradictions sometimes, and to allow people to think ill and slightingly of us, even when we do and mean well. Why do such trifles go to your heart, but because you are yet carnal and regard men more than you should. Because you are afraid of being despised, you seek shelter in excuses. If all that malice could invent were said against you, what hurt would it do you? This happened by my permission and the just man will not be troubled whatever happens him from God. Take it not to heart if some people think badly of you—you ought to think worse of yourself. For whether men put a good or bad construction on what you do, you are still what you are."

It is sometimes said that the practice of humility is not well suited to present-day conditions, and that there is need of a revision of the ascetic treatises with an eye to contemporary needs. All admit that the virtue itself, of course, is and always will be necessary but its practice as taught by the spiritual writers of other ages is not what is needed in our novitiates and seminaries today. In fact, it is averred that its practice often produces very undesirable effects, resulting at times in what amounts to a diminution of the personality. This objection is seriously made, and demands an answer.

Let us admit at once that there is some truth in it. Young men and women are to be met with who, before entering the seminary or religious life, were as bright and care-free as any of their companions, and who after a few years have become excessively reserved, silent to the point of moodiness, more or less lacking in initiative and generally exhibiting characteristics which are not those we associate with that fullness of personality that is desirable.

This state of things, if it is traceable to the practice of the traditional asceticism, notably that of humility, is due principally to lack of good direction, and not to any lack in the ascetic writers or their treatises. Humility as a virtue epitomising the whole spiritual life is strong meat. It is a virtue for the well-balanced mature man or woman, and not for the immature uncertainty of adolescence, unless guided by a good director.

While it is, apparently, true that youth is maturing earlier now than a generation ago, too much should not be made of this. It refers primarily to physical maturity. Young people nowadays are used to more freedom than formerly, and conditions of life have changed greatly since the last war. Nevertheless modern youth still remains very immature at novitiate age. There is more to maturity than being able to drive a car or order a dinner. Neither should maturity be identified with self-confidence. Modern life becomes more artificial with each passing year, and the full appointment books of the psychiatrists are evidence enough that it is not ideal for producing the " full man." The average novice needs to be prepared before being fed the strong meat of the masters, who wrote in the simpler days of the fifteenth or even the fifth century.

This applies more to humility than to the other virtues. It will be easy for a beginner to exaggerate or mis-apply statements, such as those that say simply that silence is preferable to speech, that laughter is not to be indulged in, that one should be indifferent to sickness or health. This is not for the beginner or the uninstructed. And what appear to be acts of humility can come from natural motives, such as timidity.

There is something else. Freedom and independence are in the very air we breathe today. We are all of us children of our time and milieu, much more so perhaps than we realise. That young people are not influenced by these ideas (which are, of course, excellent in themselves) is impossible. The idea of dependence is, to some extent at least, repugnant and inexplicable to them. Therefore the notion of humility does not come easily to them, partly because they do not understand it. Unaware of this, they allow their ardour and generosity to lead them into indiscretion in the practise of a virtue that calls for considerable discernment.

Further, there is great emphasis placed nowadays on self-development. The desirability of full development of the personality is continually stressed. This is inculcated in books, in lectures, in home-courses of education, and it influences the trend of formal education. It is the theme of psychologists, of child-educators, of theorists of all sorts. Initiative and drive are the qualities most admired. Once again all this is good. But too many think that humility is opposed to it all. Misunderstanding humility, they see it as opposed to all legitimate self-expression and initiative. Therefore they may develop a wrong outlook on mortification, mortifying legitimate and desirable natural tendencies. This will lead to trouble, which would be avoided by a right understanding of the virtue, but for this a certain degree of re-education is necessary.

What these generous young souls need to be taught is to practise humility with each other in the small incidents of daily life. They should be instructed in the real meaning and value of religious obedience. Their personalities need to be allowed to develop and expand in the happy family atmosphere of the novitiate, and when they have reached maturity and integration they can be led to drink deeply of the teaching of the masters. What is needed is not a revision of spirituality, but the inculcation of a right outlook, a well-balanced commonsense, and a true maturity of judgement and intellect, none of which necessarily comes with adolescence.

CHAPTER XII

HUMILITY FOR THE RELIGIOUS

At the beginning of the fifth chapter of his Rule St. Benedict makes the following statement: " The first degree of humility is ready obedience." There is something downright and dogmatic about that, that admits of no circumventing. It stands there like a great solid gateway to a city. If you want to enter, this is the way; there is no other. There is an air of finality about it. There is no getting around it.

That is as it should be. Humility consists in what we called a practical sense of the divine. It is principally concerned with the subjection of man to God. By obedience we put this subjection into immediate effect. There is little point in our reading and speaking of subjecting ourselves to God, and then refusing to do so in fact. God's principal means of manifesting his will to us is by the commands of superiors. Hence the connection between obedience and the practice of humility.

Humility inclines us to submit to other men in so far as they have something of the divine. Superiors are the visible representatives of God, having in them something of his authority. Therefore humility necessarily demands that we obey them. We obey the commands of the superior because, and in so far as, we see God in him—that is what a practical sense of the divine entails. We must recognise God wherever he manifests himself to us. He does this nowhere more clearly and unmistakeably than in the commands of authority.

As St. Catherine of Siena says: " A soul is obedient in proportion to her humility and humble in proportion to her obedience." In commenting on the text of St. Benedict given above Dom Delatte has the following to say: " The obedience of which St. Benedict speaks here is not a special degree after which there comes a second, then a third. He proclaims its sovereign value, and declares it to be the summit . . . the most complete resumé and expression of humility. Obedience and humility are so conceived by our holy father that one can be defined by the other—or better, if they are distinct it is as cause and effect, as sign and reality. Acts of obedience prepare us for and lead us to humility, that is, to be what we should be in the sight of God, and the perfection of this attitude is ready obedience."

It should be noted that the sentence above from the Rule of St. Benedict is not from the chapter on humility, the twelve degrees. It is from the chapter on obedience. So important does St. Benedict evidently consider it, that he returns to it again in his seventh chapter—the degrees. The third degree, he says, is that a monk should submit himself in all obedience to a superior, in imitation of Our Lord. The fourth degree is that if one meets with hard and contrary things, or even injuries, in the exercise of obedience, one should bear them silently and with patience. For, he says, " the Lord tries us with fire, as silver is tried in the furnace." It is generally agreed among commentators that this is the high point of the Benedictine ascesis. It has been called the " sticking point, the bridge of asses of St. Benedict's spirituality." [1] If we cross it successfully, we are well on the road to that perfect charity that is the fullness of union with God.

Why is this? It is because obedience over a long time is very difficult and mortifying. It is easy enough to submit on occasion. We may find it easy, or comparatively so, at the beginning of our religious life. But as we grow in age and experience, the practice of the virtue does not become easier. We are so proud and independent in thought and action, so confident in our own powers and judgement, that the continual state of dependence on another demanded by obedience is extremely mortifying and demands very great abnegation. This is all the more true if it is to be sustained over a long time. It will demand especially faith and humility. Faith will show us God in his representative, and humility will cause us to obey and revere that representative.

[1] Cf. Dom G. Belorgey, O.C.S.O., *L'Humilité Benedictine.*

It is evident, then, that religious obedience must be supernatural. Its aim is to unite us to the will of God. Any merely natural obedience is quite useless and indeed unworthy of a religious. Humility subjects us to what is divine in another man (in this case the divine authority) and this demands enlightened supernatural motives. It is a far cry from real religious obedience to obey a superior because he has evident qualities of mind and judgement, or because we are naturally inclined to obsequiousness or timidity, Such a manner of acting will render much of our religious life quite sterile, and will put perfection and holiness out of the question.

Obsequiousness and servility have not only no place in obedience. but they have nothing in common with true humility. In fact they are quite inimical to it. Humility is a virtue of the strong, a virtue that regards truth. Servility is a defect and a weakness that causes a man to belittle himself by submitting to another man as such. This is an unworthy procedure. For one man is as good as another and, apart from the authority which he has from God, there is no reason for submitting with the absolute universality demanded by religious obedience. Servility debases a man, but obedience based on humility elevates him. For it liberates him from such fetters as human respect, the desire to please, the timidity that is weakness. In making him dependent on God alone, it brings him the only real independence worth the name.

It is evident too how much care we should take not to evade or escape obedience in any way. If it is so mortifying, we must expect that the ego will fight to the last against it, and will seek a hundred pretexts for evading it. How easy it is, and how prone we naturally are, to rationalise motives in this matter. We cannot be too careful. St. Benedict defines the obedient monk as one who desires to have a superior over him. Such a one not merely submits to a superior, but desires to do so as a positive good. St. Catherine of Siena has the same thing to say: One who is truly obedient ever retains the desire of submission.

Obedience must be full, complete and generous. We should be convinced that it is, as St. Benedict puts it, " a boon," something to be sought rather than evaded. It is the most important practice of the religious life, and one from which nothing can dispense us. We may be unable to work, unable to attend community exercises, unable to do anything at all, but we are always able to obey.

Obedience is also the most powerful means of self-abnegation that we have. Very little experience and very little consideration of the possible extent of our generosity in it will convince us of that. Why, in fact, do we fail in obedience? Is it not essentially because of pride, of self-love manifesting itself under one form or another? For we know theoretically that the superior represents God, that therefore all we have to do is to order all our actions according to this fact. But too frequently we fail. Too frequently we evade a command; we press reasons for not carrying it out; we interpret it ungenerously; we convince ourselves that this or that was not intended; that the order does not apply to us, or does not hold under these circumstances.

It is possible to do this in all sincerity even after prayer for guidance. If a person is strong-willed and has a determined character, he will tend to identify God's will with his own. He will be prone too to interpret obedience in a way that is congenial to his own outlook and ideas. The strength of these latter and their influence over him are something he does not realise. He can quite easily believe that he is sincerely praying for light, when in fact he is merely convincing himself further on his knees before God that his ideas are the right ones, and that the command must be carried out as he wants. Exact and uncompromising obedience therefore is all the more necessary as we find ourselves of this disposition. If anyone needs humility more than another, it is the man of strong personality and conviction.

At the back of all this reasoning the fundamental lack is one of true self-abnegation. Because we love ourselves too much, because we prefer our own convenience or our own profit or ideas or judgement, we do not want to obey. If we were completely detached and if we truly desired nothing but God and his will, we should obey. Because nothing else would appear to us desirable or worth seeking. One action or duty or method of work would appear as desirable as another. The only criterion would be what had been commanded. But the death to self that this demands of us is too much for us and so we fail to obey.

On this matter of self-abnegation, Father de Guibert, S.J., has the following to say: " In the spiritual life the point which in practice is decisive, the strategic dominating position the loss or gain of which decides in effect the battle for sanctity, is abnegation. This is the point where the greater number of souls recoils, the exact point where the road forks between a life of fervour and a life of high sanctity."[2] The fervent " are pious and devout, but they have not totally died to themselves in the silence of their souls, allowing themselves to be detached from everything that is not the pure love and service of God."[3] It is this pure love that obedience will lead us to if we let it—and this is the reward of humility that St. Benedict calls perfect charity.

Our purpose is not to treat in full of the virtue of obedience. We wish only to underline its paramount importance as the principal exercise of humility for the religious, and also his principal means of progress in the virtue. For the person with religious vows, it is the absolutely necessary and fundamental practice of humility, beside which all other practices of the virtue must be only secondary.

Some may think that the outline given here refers only to the monk or nun who actually follows the Rule of St. Benedict. That is not so. It is of universal application. Abbot Marmion states that St. Benedict's teaching on obedience sets itself to destroy the very roots of self-love, and to penetrate as far as possible. It can be said therefore, that the concept of religious obedience has made no further progress as to the substance of the matter since the Holy Rule was written.[4]

The essence of obedience is that voiding of self for the possession of one's whole being by God, the practice of that state of dependence and self-denial which is the true flowering of humility. That is why humility and obedience identify themselves for the religious. In the words of St. Teresa: " Experience has taught me the inestimable advantages of obedience. In my opinion this virtue offers the quickest way to advance in the service of God. It is the most direct road to humility." (*Foundations*).

[2] *Dict. de Spiritualite*—Art. Abnegation.
[3] *Idem.*
[4] Cf. *Christ the Ideal of the Monk*, p. 263 note.

CHAPTER XIII

"A MAN SUBJECT TO AUTHORITY"

Humility is the most necessary of all the virtues. It is so at all times and for everyone. If it can be said to be more necessary for one than for another, that one is the person who is in authority. By this we mean anyone who exercises authority, not merely superiors in the strict sense. Very few of us are superiors, but many of us do have authority of one kind or another. Anyone who is placed over others has authority, and is liable to meet problems in the practical working out of humility in daily life. Perhaps it will seem difficult to reconcile the self-abnegation of humility with the strong exercise of authority that may sometimes be demanded.

There is no solution to the problem to be found in the hope that authority will never become ours. The fact is that it probably will. In one way or another it forms part of the life of almost every priest and religious. If we are teaching a class, whether of small children or fourth divines, we are exercising authority. If we are father-masters, or prefects in a college, we are in authority. If we are mistress of the school or mother bursar, dean of residence or head-gardener, we are in authority. Whether we direct the parish or the sodality or just the community cabbage-garden—in short, whenever, like the centurion in the gospel, we find ourselves in a position to say to this one " Go," and to that one " Come," we are in authority, and liable to meet problems in the exercise of humility.

We may think the word authority exaggerated when applied to some of the examples just mentioned. Yet is it not a universal experience that the king is an easier person to deal with than the palace door-keeper? There is no one more officious than the small official. However low we be on the ladder of office, we can become self-important. The lower we are, indeed, the more liable that seems to be. The petty tyranny of the minor clerk is none the less tyranny for its being petty. There is nothing more pleasant than power over others, and nothing more liable to turn the head of even a good man. It is so much more pleasing to send than to be sent, to give orders than to receive them.

The conscientious person might look for a solution in the example of the saints—or what he believes to be their example. Some of them have done all they could to avoid high office. Others have resigned their posts at the first opportunity. But someone must bear the responsibility and it would be a great mistake to think that we are imitating the humility of the saints by refusing the will of God. Refusal to accept responsibility will never sanctify us, and the timidity which is born of the wrong kind of fear is a poor foundation for grace to build on. For authority is an integral element of the Church of God, and the classless society is as utopian in the sphere of religion and the spirit as it is in that of economics and politics. Superiors and subjects there must be, teachers and pupils, masters and disciples, principals and assistants, centurions and private soldiers.

In this as in all else Our Lord has shown us how to act, and has set the example. Indeed in this more than in most matters he has gone out of his way to teach us. On one occasion there was a strife among the apostles as to which of them should be greatest. And Jesus, calling them, said to them: " You know that they who rule over the Gentiles, lord it over them, and their princes have power over them. But it is not so among you, but whoever shall be the greater shall be your minister, and whoever shall be the first among you shall be the servant of all. For the Son of Man is not come to be ministered unto, but to minister."

There are two points to be noted in this passage. Firstly Our Lord does not exclude authority or its exercise from his kingdom. Secondly that authority is to be exercised as he exercised it, and not as the gentile princes do. Authority in the strict canonical sense belongs only to properly constituted superiors. But we need not restrict the principle to these. It remains valid for all authority, even when taken at its broadest, i.e. whenever a man finds himself placed over others, whoever they be. The principle is that all authority must be exercised as a loving service, a ministering to those under us. What Christ condemns is the egoistical abuse of authority, a lording it over others. In reality, we are never less ourselves than when placed over others, and no one would have power if it were not given him from above.

To speak of " my " power or " my " authority is simply pride.

Because it is not mine. I am given it by God that I may use it for the building up of the Mystical Body in charity. All authority, all power over others, is born of love, the love of Christ for his chosen people, the souls he has redeemed. If we act as though it were born of personal superiority over others, or allow it to issue in domination or seeking for personal service, we become an obstacle to the action of God on souls, instead of being an instrument of that action. In external results, in order maintained, in work accomplished, we may appear very efficient and leave nothing to be desired. But it cannot be believed that through us the power of God, and the influence of Christ, are making themselves felt on souls. Despite us, rather than because of us, will souls be sanctified and led to God. We must always keep before us the principle given above—that all authority is essentially a loving service of others. Only by so doing shall we ensure that we never err in its use.

For it immediately becomes evident that we must always consult the good of others. Now that good may demand that we come to them with a rod, as St. Paul did to the Corinthians. Or it may demand that we say, " Neither will I condemn thee," and dismiss them in peace. For example, to neglect to enforce discipline in a class or among those committed to our care; to allow scandal to be given when we could stop it; to fail to condemn and so to seem to condone wrong-doing or misbehaviour is not consulting the good of others. Again to allow human respect, or plain weakness, to prevent us from exercising strictness where it is called for is not to serve the good of those under us. If we act so, we are failing completely in humility, because we are failing to act as God's instrument. In other words we are asserting ourselves. And that is so even though, paradoxically, we may appear to be failing to assert ourselves. What we are really failing to assert is God's rights and the demands of the good.

This point is important. If we allow ourselves to think that humility demands that we never put our foot down, that we never speak out in sharp and definite admonition, we are dismissing the virtue as being of no practical consequence in life. To act thus is manifestly foolish—chaos would be the result. So we subconsciously conclude that there is something impractical about humility, and where there is a job to be done, a class to be looked after, a group to be directed, we need more active virtue. To think in this way is to show that we completely misunderstand humility, but it is a misunderstanding that is all too common.

In reality, the humble man is the only one fit for authority. He alone will always have God's rights and his own duties before his eyes, and so will never fail those under his charge. He will realise that he has been given authority in order that he may serve those over whom he presides, whatever that will entail. He will neither make the exercise of obedience a burden by his own short-comings and smallness, nor condone wrong-doing by his weakness and indecision. He will not fear to speak out boldly and decisively if there be need, remembering that the shepherd is responsible for the sheep. He will not seek special privilege, nor let the image of God in him be dimmed for others by pompousness and egoism. He will not arrogate to himself an authority that is not his. With no one more than with himself will he make the necessary distinction between the man and the office.

In this way he will realise that although he is himself no better than those under him, for we are all brethren and one is our master, his office demands that he lead and correct them. But likewise this duty of correction is something divine, which belongs to his office and not at all to himself as a person. He will remember that while he is himself a sinner like all men, he is bound, because of the authority which is his, to bring Christ to other men, and to serve the building up of the Body of Christ by this authority. He will never allow his own weakness to weaken charity. Neither will he mistake a natural forthrightness for zeal. He will not hesitate to demand that others honour Christ in himself, but neither will he allow himself to obscure the vision of Christ for others. He will remember that Our Lord washed the feet of his disciples, but also that he was consumed by zeal for his Father's glory; that he rebuked the apostles when they sought the first places; but that he made a scourge of little cords and drove the money changers from the Temple, overturning their tables; that Christ's anger was ever born of his regard for the rights of God, and not of his own dignity or sensitiveness.

In short, where the man who lacks humility will fail in the exercise of authority, falling into either weakness or a type of arrogance, the truly humble man will be the successful teacher, leader, superior or director. His use of authority will be a service of others. He will realise that that service demands both gentleness and firmness, abnegation and assertion—abnegation of himself and assertion of the rights of God. Further, only the humble man will fulfil the duties of office with that charity and ease, which will earn the respect and affection of those under him, since he alone thinks nothing of himself. Only humility will give that purity of intention that is so necessary, because it alone frees a man from all ambition and makes him truly disinterested.

Finally, only the humble man will be conscious that nowhere more than in the exercise of authority is the guidance of God needed through the gift of counsel and light on the duties of his state. He will never make the mistake of thinking that he can handle any and every situation without first having recourse to God in prayer. His humility will lead to his asking that he may neither break the bruised reed through his natural strength of character, nor fail to drive the money changers from the Temple, because of weakness or desire for favour.

Therefore, while it is in no way to be expected that those in authority should publicly humiliate themselves in a manner that may be useful for others, it is of the utmost importance that their exercise of authority be impregnated with humility. Such humility will be born of love, and will issue in as genuine and as full a respect for those under their charge as they themselves expect and demand from their subjects.

CHAPTER XIV

AMBITION

THE derivation of the word " ambition " is interesting. It comes from an old Latin word used to describe the activity of a candidate for office in ancient Rome who went about canvassing for votes among the influential. It is no longer used in this sense, but the idea remains much the same. The ambitious man is one who is much concerned about getting himself into office.

Ambition can be good of course. We call a man ambitious if he wants to get on in his job, wants to improve himself, to better his condition. That is admirable and to be commended. We are not concerned with it here. There is another kind of ambition. The dictionary puts it neatly: "It can also be inordinate, and in that case it is that excessive desire for honour, preferment, superiority and power." It is a temptation that most experience, and it is hardly necessary to say that it is opposed to humility.

There is little that a man will more quickly believe about himself than that he is superior to others. Nothing is easier than to think that because we are naturally of a dominant disposition and character, strong-willed and forceful in personality, able to express our ideas and opinions, that we are therefore born leaders. Because it is in every man to prefer himself to others, it is likewise in him, at least in principle, to want to be in charge of others. To assume that one is superior to others leads quickly and almost imperceptibly to a desire for superiority in externals—that is for actual superiority. That is ambition for power.

We do not put it that way. It appears to us, and perhaps others have said it, that we are fitted to hold positions of authority. In fact, it seems fair to say that we could fill these positions as well if not better, in some respects at least, than those who are now in office. A desire to lead others is not in itself bad. That is true. But only on condition that that desire springs from a right motive and a pure intention. Too often it does not.

There are few of us who are not really convinced in our hearts that we are cut out to hold posts of responsibility. If a friend says to us: " You know you would make a good superior "—what is our reaction? We laughingly deprecate it: " Me? Not at all, don't be silly." But inside we feel a pleasing glow, and we are impressed that at least one person recognises capability when he sees it. " Mind you, it's not that I say I'd be another St. Benedict or St. Teresa, but I'd do as well as anyone else. And there are a few things I would like to fix up."

If the matter goes no further than that, we may say it is not so bad. But we are called to perfection and holiness, not to a state of being " not so bad." Holiness does not consist merely in avoiding the greater " sins, but in coming to the closest union with God. And we have seen that this union can be achieved only in the depths of nothingness which is perfect humility. It is, to some extent, an uncharted dark mysterious place—the Nada of St. John of the Cross—and of ourselves we can force our spirit only to its frontiers. Then it recoils at the final annihilation of losing itself in the darkness on the mountain top. But this is the darkness that surrounds the throne of God, and into it we must penetrate if we would possess him. If we go so far, God himself will bring us the remainder of the way, and lead us into that light which is darkness to us, because we are not yet pure enough to look on it and not be blinded. The essential formula of this journey to the mountain top is: " Love to be unknown and esteemed as nothing "—not: " I would be as good as anyone else in office, if I got the chance." This latter is nature's reaction, it is the first strivings of ambition. The former is grace, God calling us to himself. That the Church realises the possibility of our not always acting according to the grace of God and his call to perfection is clear from the Canon Law. She does all that prudence can suggest to ensure that elections and appointments of superiors will be free and above board. There are oaths to be taken, statements to be made, votes to be examined, prohibitions against seeking votes to be observed. Every attempt is made to ensure that even if we think we are the best candidate for the job, we will put someone else into it. We always, of course, apply all this to others, complacently thinking that it could not apply to us. Why not? We are all descended from the same tainted source. There go I but for the grace of God.

St. Bernard regards ambition as the third temptation, the first being lust and the second vainglory. Only if these are unavailing in bringing down the spiritual man does the devil have recourse to ambition. In other words it is precisely a temptation of the strong: " So he (the devil) says to himself, 'It is plain to me now that I cannot succeed by open force; but perhaps I may be able to gain my object by craft, with the traitor to help me.' Who do you think is this traitor? The traitor is ambition, that subtle evil, that secret poison, that hidden pest, that deviser of mischief, that mother of hypocrisy, that parent of envy, that fountain of sin, that instigator of crimes, that rust of the virtues, that moth of sanctity, that blindness of hearts, that vice which changes even remedies into maladies, and uses medicine to produce disease. 'He has despised vainglory,' says the tempter, 'because it is vain. Perhaps he will accept something more solid, perhaps he will accept honours or pleasures.' Oh, how many has not this caused to be cast into the exterior darkness of hell, having first deprived them of their wedding garment, and robbed their virtuous practices of all the fruits of piety. What numbers has not this pest wickedly supplanted and shamefully cast down, so that all others who had not suspected the presence of that which secretly saps virtue, were struck with

terror at their sudden fall . . . how empty is the consolation of
earthly honours, how heavy the judgement that awaits them, how
short a time will they remain with us, and how uncertain their
ending!" [1]

There is a story in the *Book of Judges* which forms a living
example of the contrast between the humble man and the proud
ambitious seeker after office. The story is that of Gideon and
Abimelech.[2] The people of Israel had disobeyed God and he had
delivered them up to the Madianites in punishment. These
oppressed and persecuted them " so that there was nothing left
in all Israel for sustenance of life,' whether of man or beast. For
the Madianites came like locusts, an innumerable multitude of
them, filling all places and wasting everything. And Israel cried
to God for help. So he sent his angel to Gideon, who was preparing
to flee from Madian, and Gideon complained to him that God
had abandoned Israel. Then the Lord said to him: ' Go, and thou
shalt deliver Israel out of the hand of Madian, for I have sent
thee'." Now see the answer of humility: " Wherewith shall I
deliver Israel? Behold my family is the meanest in Manasses and
I am the least in my father's house." He could not visualise himself
as leader of the people. When God assures him that he will be with
him, Gideon asks for a sign that he may know he is not deceived.
Not a lack of faith but rather a rooted conviction of his own
unworthiness and incapacity that prompted his hesitation. God did
not reprimand him, but gave him the sign he asked—the dew on
the fleece.

Convinced then that it was God's will that he should lead the
nation, Gideon accepted the office to which God called him, and
by the power of God delivered Israel from servitude. We need
not recapitulate the remainder of the story. You will find it in the
Book of Judges. With only three hundred men he defeated the
Madianites, destroying them utterly. Even at the height of his
victory his humility shone forth. " For the men of Israel said to
him: 'Rule thou over us'; but he said: 'I will not, neither will my
son, but the Lord himself will rule over you.' And the land rested
while Gideon presided." Now look at the other figure, his son
Abimelech, a man full of ambition and lust for power. As soon
as his father dies, he proclaims that it is better that he should rule

[1] *Sermon 6 on Psalm* 90.   [2] *Judges*, chaps. 6–9.

the people of Sichem than that his brethren should. So he forth-
with sets upon these latter and kills them all. He takes command
of the people, and for a while it seems he is going to be successful.
His wars prosper, he defeats his enemies. But God is biding his
time. Abimelech leads his forces against Thebes and is killed by
a Theban woman. Note the sentence that follows: " God repaid
the evil that Abimelech had done against his father, slaying his
brethren." God repaid the evil. Ambition led him to do it in the
first place, and God allowed him to have his way for a while. Then
he repaid the evil for Abimelech had had his reward. A man aspires
to office for the glory it brings him, for the superiority, the power,
the selfish desire for pre-eminence. He gets it. Has he not received
his reward? God will repay him, for he has done evil.

Ambition, unlike the other passions, does not weaken with age.
It can lead a man into all sorts of offences against God and his
neighbour. And it effectively and completely rules out that perfection of charity to which God calls us, for it is essentially selfish,
seeking the glory of men rather than that of God. As St. Teresa
puts it: " Honour itself is lost by seeking it, especially in desiring
high posts of honour, for there is no poison in the world which so
effectively destroys perfection. . . . If anyone hearkens after
honours though he may have spent many years in prayer, or
rather in speculation (for true prayer removes these defects) he
will never make any progress nor enjoy the fruit of prayer . . .
Our honour ought to consist in serving God." [3]

Preferment, like much else that is good, is dangerous for us
in our fallen state. Indeed it is the more dangerous in that the wound
of pride is the deeper. St. Paul says that to desire office is to desire
a good thing. The thing itself is good, but we are not. It is not
merely that power corrupts—we are corrupt already without it.

" To be humble in abjection is nothing very great; but it is
great virtue indeed, and as rare as great, to be humble in the midst
of honours. For instance, were the Church, deceived by my
hypocrisy, to advance such a miserable wretch as I to some post
of honour, even though not very exalted, God permitting this either
on account of my own sins or because of the sins of those under me,
should I not immediately forget what I really am and begin to
suppose myself such as I am reputed by men, who cannot see

[3] Chapters 12 and 13 of *The Way of Perfection* should be read.

the heart? Undoubtedly, I should give credit to public opinion, and turn a deaf ear to the voice of conscience. And estimating virtue by honour, not honour by virtue, I should account myself the more holy in proportion as I should find myself elevated above others." [4]

But there is a further reason for fearing and abhorring ambition in ourselves. The ideal of the spiritual life is to deliver ourselves up completely to the demands of charity. Note the word "completely." For the priest or religious, this ideal finds its fulfilment in being God's and his alone. *Pars mea Deus*, God is my portion. We must be content with God, and find our all in him. Therefore if we find ambition taking hold of us, it very likely indicates a divided heart.

This is so, not merely in the same way that any temptation might make us doubt our purity of intention. Ambition shows that we are not content with God alone, that he does not satisfy us, and that our heart is seeking something else in hunger. Not only is perfection outlawed by ambition, but ambition is itself a pointer that our love of God is not what we profess it to be. We have renounced creatures but we have not cleaved to God, and so our spirit is reaching blindly for something else. Either we give all to God and find fulfilment in him, or we do not, and so set up an inner conflict in ourselves that can lead to dreadful selfishness. And even if we satisfy this selfishness, it must be at the cost of hearing at the end those words of Christ: "You have had your reward."

[4] St. Bernard, *Sermon 4 on the Glories of the Virgin Mother.*

CHAPTER XV

APPROACH TO THE VIRTUE

T HE virtue of humility cannot be obtained by a simple process of " Do this " and " Avoid that." If it could, a set of rules would be the most necessary conclusion to this book. Humility is essentially an attitude of soul—the attitude of the creature in the presence of God, what we called a practical sense of the divine.

A variety of factors will help to develop and deepen this attitude in us. Some of these are themselves acts of the virtue of humility, others more properly lead to and intensify it. We have already dealt with some of them. In this and the following chapters we will discuss a few that seem to be the most important and effective.

Recall what we have already said—that humility is essentially and fundamentally reverence for God and his works. There is no other adequate basis for the virtue. If we try to build on self-knowledge alone we are likely to end up in discouragement. Merely natural motives, such as the fact that no one is indispensable, will not of themselves lead to humility. They may help, but the virtue is founded on something else. Only grace and the practice of supernatural virtue will bring us to God.

" There is a kind of humility which truth produces in us, and which is without warmth, as there is also another kind which is produced and warmed by charity. The one has its seat in knowledge, the other in the will. If you look into yourself in the light of truth, and without dissimulation, and judge yourself unflatteringly, there is no doubt that you will be humbled, even in your own eyes; and this true knowledge of yourself will render you more vile in your own sight, although perhaps you cannot as yet endure that this be so with others. You will then be humble, but as yet only by the effect of truth, and not by the infusion of love. . . . You see then that it is not the same thing whether a man being constrained by light and knowledge, has a lowly opinion of himself, and whether he is helped by the grace of charity, and willingly accepts a humble position; for the one is forced, the other voluntary." [1]

[1] St. Bernard, *Sermon 42 on the Canticle.*

The most important and efficacious means of acquiring and advancing in humility is prayer. St. Thomas says that we acquire humility *primo et principaliter per donum gratiae*, first and above all by the gift of grace. There is, consequently, no adequate substitute for prayer. If we do not pray, that is, endeavour by the constant practice of mental prayer to unite ourselves to God, we shall not be humble. Abbot Marmion points out that if God, even once in prayer, gave us to realise something of his greatness, the essential groundwork of the virtue would be laid, and by preserving this divine illumination an intense spirit of reverence would grow in our souls.

This teaching of the great Benedictine is of first importance, for it underlines the essence of the virtue in a single phrase. A divine light on the greatness of God, received even once in prayer, is the essential ground-work. The basis of the virtue is neither self-knowledge, nor a low opinion of oneself, nor a preference of others to oneself, nor self-depreciation. It is simply and solely a realisation of the greatness of God. This leads to reverence which is the root and principle of humility.

An illumination of this kind in prayer is not something extra-ordinary, something reserved for those who are in the highest stages of mystical prayer. The proof of this lies in Marmion's own life. He recorded in his diary that he himself received just such an illumination one day when as a seminary student he was entering the classroom. To the person who is faithful to prayer and generous in his life, God does give these lights. It would be a mistake to think they are a privilege of the few.

We have already seen how St. John of the Cross ascribes the uprooting of all thought of our own superiority over others to advance in prayer. It is not a mere intellectual conviction that we seek. Humility is not the result of syllogistic reasoning. It comes to a man on his knees in prayer, for it is a grace. Prayer should transform us, in our outlook and in our way of judging. To prefer ourselves to others is deep in us, and only the transforming effect of true prayer will rid us of it. If we still find ourselves passing judgement on others after many years spent in the practice of mental prayer, it is a sign that our prayer has been speculation rather than true prayer, as St. Teresa says.

The point here raised by St. John is important. You cannot acquire humility out of a book. A book can teach you a certain amount about it. But the virtue is only acquired in prayer and in the bitter experience of oneself. And in order that this latter be useful to teach and not merely to depress, prayer is necessary. Our poverty and inadequacy come home to us on our knees in the presence of God. Otherwise their realisation may well only embitter. Accepted rightly, our failings will teach us more humility in a quarter of an hour before the tabernacle than will the reading of a life-time. Prayer then is the basic and essential means. Without it all our other efforts will be more or less useless. " Unless the Lord build the house, they labour in vain who build it."

We should also constantly ask God to enlighten us on our need of this virtue, and to give us increase of it. An excellent litany for this purpose will be found in the life of Marmion. We must however take care that in using formulae such as these, we do not allow them to become mere words. A great sincerity is needed in their use, and a full and generous co-operation with grace, by accepting all the humiliations that come to us. There will be little point in praying that God would deliver us from the desire of being praised, and then allowing ourselves to be upset because we are not in fact praised. Prayers like these can easily become a meaningless substitute for the practice of solid virtue. When using them, we must try and develop at the same time the " unprofitable-servant " attitude. Then there will be a reciprocal causality between our lives and our prayers, and we can be certain of the help of grace.

If meditation on the greatness and perfections of God is the principal means of progress in humility, it may be asked what about self-knowledge? Should we make no effort to come to know ourselves? To think so would be a mistake. What we must avoid is a too self-conscious turning in on ourselves, a concentration on our defects and weaknesses, which would not lead to holiness. Studied thinking about oneself is not to be encouraged, and will not help. God is the only worthy object of our contemplation, and we ourselves are not worth thinking about.

There is one precious means of self-knowledge which we should make the most of, and that is frequent confession. In his Encyclical on the Mystical Body Pope Pius XII says that " by means of frequent confession the right knowledge of oneself is increased, and progress is made in Christian humility." So important did he, evidently, consider the point that he returned to it again in his

Exhortation to the Priests of the World—*Menti Nostrae*—and repeated the passage from the encyclical. This authoritative statement of the Pope puts the matter beyond the realm of a mere recommendation, or the idea of an individual. The use of frequent confession is given us here with Papal authority as an excellent means of progress in humility.

In order that this be realised in practice, two things are necessary. Firstly, all semblance of routine must be avoided, and secondly, the confession must be made with great discernment and sincerity. Routine will inevitably put all real progress out of the question. It brings perfunctoriness in examination and accusation; boredom, remissness in performing penance; and half-hearted sorrow. It may eventually lead to disgust. Actually the intention of using the sacrament as a means of growth in humility will itself be an excellent preventive of routine.

Secondly, we must confess our sins with discernment. This demands that we examine our conscience with care, seeking the underlying motives of our sins, and the real reasons for our repeated falls into the same faults. In place of simply confessing lies, for example, we must see why we tell lies. What will be needed is to see why we tell lies . . . from motives of vanity, human respect, convenience. Without this, our examination and accusation will become perfunctory, and of little real use for the purpose we are discussing.

Spiritual direction will be very helpful here, and care should be taken in the choice of a confessor, if that is possible. It would be as well to discuss the matter with him, to ensure his co-operation. If we do this, and are in earnest about it, results are assured. It will not be possible to go to confession weekly and not advance in knowledge of our own weakness and need of God's sustaining grace and help.[2]

Allied to confession is our daily examen of conscience. We must not allow this to become a painful probing of the soul. If we find ourselves becoming at all scrupulous or over-anxious, we should seek advice, and turn our attention more fully to God. Our sinfulness must never turn to despair or discouragement. It should rather cause us to cast ourselves on God's merciful love, to come to an ever greater realisation of our need of Him, and an ever greater

---

[2] *Pardon and Peace*, by A. Wilson, C.P., will be helpful.

appreciation of how true it is that we can do nothing without Him. Frequent confession should lead us to this. If used rightly it will be the great means of self-knowledge. It has inestimable advantages over other practices of self-examination in that it is always accompanied, because of the sacrament, by divine grace and light. So we shall receive precisely the graces we need most, particularly a realisation of our sinfulness.

We have already spoken about external acts of humiliation. Owing to the ease with which we can deceive ourselves in this matter, we should never impose these on ourselves. If we feel strongly moved by grace to do so, we should consult our director beforehand and be guided by his advice. There are few practices in the spiritual life more likely to lead to self-deception than undertaking humiliations of our own choice. But this must not make us lose sight of the fact that humiliation is absolutely necessary for growth in humility. As reading is the way to knowledge, says St. Bernard, so is humiliation the way to humility. But humiliation must be accepted rightly. Otherwise it will merely embitter us. Whenever we are humiliated, either by our own faults or mistakes, or by being misjudged by others, or treated unfairly, we must try to accept gladly and freely. This will not be easy, especially at first, but a continued tendency to complain and justify ourselves is a sure sign that we have no real humility.

" How many are humiliated who are not humble. Some are bitter and grudging because they are humiliated; others bear it with patience; others even with willingness. The first are blameworthy, the second blameless, the last holy. He who is able to say, 'It is good for me that thou hast humbled me,' is truly humble. He who bears humiliation unwillingly cannot say this, much less he who murmurs at it. To neither of these is grace promised because he is humiliated . . . since it is not to the humiliated that God gives grace but to the humble. It is perfect and joyful humility which alone deserves the grace of God . . . that which is constrained or forced . . . will not have grace on account of the sorrow and regret mingled with it . . . such a one does not endure his humiliation willingly or gladly—it is not he who is merely humiliated who is exalted, but he who willingly and cheerfully accepts humiliation . . . although the material part of humility is supplied by another person, e.g. through reproaches, losses or sufferings, still one cannot rightly be said to be humbled by another in the same sense in which he humbles himself, when he resolves to suffer all these things with joyful and quiet mind, because they are the will of God." [3]

We should not ordinarily desire contempt or derision, but we should try to be indifferent to praise. Especially when we are wrong must we be ready to admit it. This is elementary virtue indeed, but it is very, very difficult. Make no mistake about it—the bitterest words you will ever be called upon to say are the three little words: " I was wrong."

Be ready to admit yourself at fault if you are blamed. But even if you are not at fault, you can use these small occasions for practising virtue. Remember the story about St. Thomas when he was wrongly " corrected " while reading in the refectory. He immediately re-read the sentence, mispronouncing the word. When asked afterwards why he had done so, he replied that humility is more important than the length of a syllable.

Perhaps you will say that if we do this we may become proud of our efforts, and they will be defeated. That is possible. The thing to do then is to make an act of humility, reflecting how silly we are to be proud of such a trifle. And then perhaps we will be proud of this? And so it will go on and on. If this happens, laugh at yourself and forget all about it. We must use commonsense in our spiritual life, and never lose our sense of humour.

There is one further point. It may appear that the practices we have given here will lead to self-consciousness to an undesirable degree. Is that so? No, not if they are used sensibly and with prudence. Remember especially that they are only means. If they assume the importance of ends the results will certainly be undesirable. If they degenerate into fetishes so that a man is afraid to omit them, and fears that if he does so he will be committing sins of pride, they have become harmful. But that is evidently because such a one has not understood the real nature of humility at all. If a particular practice cannot be used without leading to self-consciousness, it had better be dropped. Hence the need for maturity that we have stressed before, or else for careful direction.

In conclusion, we cannot improve on the words of St. Bernard: "With regard to all this question (that of ascending by humility and descending by pride), you will learn more about it in your own heart, by actually trying the ascent, than in all the words of our treatise." [4]

[3] St. Bernard, *Sermon* 34 *on the Canticle.*
[4] *Of the Degrees of Humility.*

CHAPTER XVI

HE WAS REPUTED WITH
THE WICKED

O NE of the benefits of the Incarnation, according to
St. Augustine, is that is gives us an example of humility on the
part of God that is calculated to show up and destroy our pride.
He goes on to note that this pride is the greatest obstacle that keeps
man back from God,[1] and asks again, what pride is there that will
not be healed by the humiliation of the Son of God.[2]

The humility of Christ is indeed the cause of the healing of our
pride in that it led him to Calvary and so to the work of our
redemption. For he humbled himself, becoming obedient unto
death, even unto the death of the cross. His humility made him
submit to the cross. On the night before he died, he summed up
the inspiration of his life as love: " That the world may know that
I love the Father, as the Father hath given me commandment so
do I." But this loving acceptance of the Father's will worked itself
out in humility. For it led him to become one of us, a sinner to
all appearances, and to submit willingly and fully to the condition
of sinners. " He who alone was without a wound disdained not
to wear the bandages of the wounded." (St. Bernard).

Neither the lowly external conditions of his life, nor his material
poverty constituted the humility of Our Lord. These things can
exist without humility. While they may lead to it, on the other hand
they may not, and anyhow are only external circumstances. Neither
was it the humiliation of his death, that of a criminal, that was the
essence of Christ's humility. The same can be said for it. It was
rather the fact that he freely chose to submit himself to these things,
and accepted them although there was no need for him to do so.

This must be clearly understood. As God, Christ could not have
humility. But as man he could, even though he knew himself to
be the Son of God. Being God he was also man, and like to us

[1] *De Trin.*, xvii: 13.   [2] *De Agon. Christ*, xi:12.

in all things. And this was because he willed it. His humility differed from ours in that it could not be that of a redeemed sinner. He could not say of himself that he was an unworthy servant. Alone of all he was the one supremely worthy servant, for everything he did was infinitely pleasing to his Father. But his humility was none the less real for this.

When the Word assumed human nature, he could have come gloriously and impassibly. He could have enjoyed the gift of integrity, as did Adam before the Fall, so that nothing could hurt or affect him. He did not do so, because he willed to appear on earth exactly as other men. St. Thomas Aquinas has the following to say: " Christ could have assumed this power (integrity) if he had wished. But since man has three states—glory, innocence and sin—he assumed something from each . . . from the state of sin he assumed the necessity of being under the penalties of this life." [3] " Glory flows into the body from the soul . . . but this natural relation in Christ was subject to the will of his Godhead, and thereby it came to pass that the beatitude remained in his soul, and was not shared in by the body, but the flesh suffered what belongs to a passible nature . . . it was by the consent of the divine will that the flesh was allowed to suffer and to do what belonged to it." [4] " Since Christ assumed human nature without sin, he might have assumed the nature without its penalties. But he wished to bear its penalties in order to carry out the work of our redemption." [5]

Our Lord, therefore, accepted these results of sin, not because they were his due as they are ours, but because it was his Father's will. All the ills that come upon us, whether from circumstances, or from other men, their malice, their envy, their thoughtlessness, are a result of sin. God wills them in so far as he allows them. In creating a world in which men would be free, he created one in which these things would be possible. Because of our loss of integrity, and because of the malice of other men, we suffer. Suffering makes up a great part of every human life. To rebel against it is, in the end, to rebel against God who allows it. It is further to seek and demand for ourselves a condition that does not belong to us. It is to demand for ourselves the state of innocence. But we are sinners and therefore this is pride.

Christ, on the other hand, is not a sinner. He could have enjoyed

[3] III, q. 13, a 3, ad 2.   [4] Ibid., q. 14, a 1, ad 2.
[5] Ibid., a 3, ad 1.

integrity so that the malice of men should not touch him. He never did so, because he never claimed that his lot should be different from ours.

We must not think of Our Lord's life as so pre-arranged by his Father that it worked itself out effortlessly to its climax. Once the Incarnation had taken place he became exactly as the rest of us, in being subject to secondary causes, to circumstances and to events. The great happenings of his life were all the result of such secondary causes. But behind these the plan of God was working out and the prophecies were being fulfilled.

The apparently accidental timing of the decree of Augustus brought Our Lady to Bethlehem for the birth of Christ. The malice of Herod precipitated the flight to Egypt, and only on the death of Herod did Palestine become safe for the Holy Family. Fear of Archelaus in Judea made Joseph select Nazareth of Galilee as a dwelling place. Each one of these events was the result of a created secondary cause. Each was to some extent painful and troublesome to Christ. He objected to none of them, used his divine power to change none of them. For he saw in them the will of his Father. He had chosen the condition of a sinner in a sinful world. This was what this condition led to. Therefore he embraced it, and the will of God for the redemption of man worked itself out, and the prophecies were fulfilled.

The submission of Christ to the providence of God in these things was truly extraordinary. They typify exactly the providential indications of God's will that irk us most, that we rebel against and grumble at, that make the greatest demands on our humility. Yet for us their acceptance is the merest justice, for we are sinners. No matter what happens to us, we can never say we deserved better. But that was not so with Christ. His humility lay in accepting these things without his deserving them.

He never complained, never repined, never gave up. He went ahead through his whole life, right up to the end, allowing the malice of men, their thoughtlessness and their obtuseness, to work against him. He never tried to avert this by using his divine power, he never said that it should not be so. There is a quality about Our Lord that looks something like fatalism. He goes ahead, indifferent to the circumstances of his life in that he never rebels against them. This is not fatalism but humility. It is the result of Christ saying to himself: I have come into a sinful world, in the condition of a sinner, among sinful men. Therefore I will suffer as a sinner. As I have taken this condition on myself I will accept its consequences.

The examples and incidents we have given are all connected with the childhood of Our Lord, but conditions were never different at any time during his life. He constantly met failure, misunderstanding and reproach. The malice of the Pharisees and priests led to the final persecution that issued in his death. He had no need to undergo all this, apart from the Father's will, but he obeyed that will even unto death. He did this not only in the sense that he obeyed the eternal decree of the Redemption and therefore of the Passion, but also in the sense that he obeyed the Father's will as manifested in the circumstances of his life. He did so consistently and without fail, even when it meant suffering.

Take, for instance, the various rejections Our Lord endured, as told us by the Evangelists. He foresaw all of these, and knew they would follow his actions with this group of people or in these circumstances, yet he never hesitated to submit to them. There is the rejection at the outset of his mission: Is not this Jesus, whose father and mother we know? There is the rejection by those disciples who refused to accept the promise of the Eucharist and walked no more with him. There is the attempt to stone him, the accusation that he cast out devils by the power of the devil, the implication of his consorting with publicans and sinners, that he was a sinner himself.

The list could be lengthened, but none of these compares with the rejections of the Passion. The terrible one of the mob outside the palace of Pilate: We have no king but Caesar. Christ, the Prophet-King, had come and his people rejected him. Repudiating their history and the traditions of their ancestors, harking back across the dim past of the centuries that were gone, to the day on which God had spoken to Samuel, they rejected him. " Give them a king to rule over them," said God to Samuel, " for they have not rejected you but me, that I should not rule over them." Now God had come, in very deed they repeated the scene: " We have no king but Caesar."

And Pilate asked them which would they that he release unto them, Jesus or Barrabas who was a murderer. But they cried: Barrabas. And Pilate released to them the murderer, but Jesus he delivered up to be crucified. This was the reaction of his people to the Saviour.

Then as he hung on the Cross came the last word from the leaders of the people: If thou be the Son of God, come down from the Cross. In face of this profound and terrible suffering we must remind ourselves again that it was the events of Christ's life, working themselves out as do the events of every man's, that brought him to this. In addition, he foresaw and could have avoided it. His acceptance of these events was the obedience that led him to Calvary and rejection and death. It could have been different. He was God. He was without sin. But he willed to be like us in everything else—he was reputed with the wicked. Being born into a world of sin, in which men were free, he accepted all the consequences. As a result he has become, not the unworthy servant, but the suffering servant.

" So shall his face be inglorious among men . . . there is no beauty in him nor comeliness and we have seen him . . . despised and the most abject of men, a man of sorrows and acquainted with infirmity, his look hidden and despised. Whereupon we esteemed him not . . . he was offered because it was his own will and he opened not his mouth." (*Isaias* 53).

In the light of all this it is evident that humility was in a sense the " form " of all Christ's actions.[6] Humility is the unifying element running through them all that gives them coherence, consistency and a pattern. Humility with him is not one virtue to be called into play on occasion. It is the stuff of which his attitude to life is made. It is the great force enabling him to see and accept the Father's will in all the circumstances of his life. Charity led him to do it: That the world may know that I love the Father. But humility is the virtue that shines out in the actual doing of it—because it was all, in great measure, an accepting, an enduring, a passion.

To understand the humility of Christ it is not enough to take isolated acts of his and propose them to oneself as examples to be imitated. It goes deeper than that. His attitude to the providential working out of the Divine Plan in his life shows the essential humility of Christ. It can be traced all through his actions—the poverty and hardship of his lot, his subjection to his creatures, his obedience to Mary and Joseph. The instances we have given are only instances. But the unifying element in Christ's reaction to them all is his humility.

---

[6] Note that St. Bernard calls humility " the characteristic virtue of Christ." (*Ser.* 1 *for Epiphany*).

But did Our Lord really mean to give us an example of humility by his life, or are the incidents we have outlined examples of the virtue in a sort of accidental fashion? The answer to this is to be found in his admonition to the Apostles. They had already served under him for a considerable time, and yet were still arguing about the first places in the Kingdom. This desire for superiority was not confined to James and John or to their mother. All the apostles were infected by it. Hearing them dispute about it, Our Lord was able to see that they had not learned the essential lesson. So he took a little child and set him in the midst of them, and told them that unless they became as little children they could not enter the Kingdom of Heaven.

That is a categoric statement, and, coming as it does from the lips of Christ himself, it can be taken as the supreme justification of the necessity for humility. For what is this childlikeness that he commands? It is humility. We realise that we are completely dependent on God, as a child is on its parents. We owe him everything and we can do nothing of ourselves. Therefore we order all our lives and all our actions according to this truth, accepting everything that comes to us from the hand of our heavenly Father. We recognise that we deserve nothing, and therefore we are happy with whatever God sends us.

The effort to practise this will show us the depths of conversion it implies, for our pride and self-sufficiency go very deep. But if we do make the effort, it will bring us to that poverty of spirit that St. Thérèse called spiritual childhood, and which enabled her to say at the end: " Yes, I have understood humility." To it and to it alone, Christ promised possession of the Kingdom: Unless you become as little children, you shall not enter. And the most powerful motive we shall find for its practice is the humility of Our Lord's own life. This is the point stressed in the Church's prayer for humility. The Collect " For Humility " in the Missal runs: " O God who dost resist the proud and give grace to the humble, grant us the virtue of true humility, of which Thine Only Son showed himself an example to the faithful . . . " Our humility must be modelled on that of Christ. For, as St. Bernard says, how can man do other than humble himself in the presence of a humble God?

CHAPTER XVII

THE MASS AS AN
EXPRESSION OF HUMILITY

Since the Mass is the centre of Christian life, it will be closely connected with the fundamental virtue of humility. Its immediate connection with it through the virtue of religion is evident. Religion inclines us to worship God as we ought, leading us especially to offer him the supreme act of worship which is sacrifice.

This act of sacrifice is the most " creaturely " of acts, in that it expresses and epitomises the desire and yearning of man for God, and his recognition of God's greatness. Man recognises that he is a creature, that he needs God, that he depends on him and owes all to him. Therefore he immediately bows down in adoration, petition and thanksgiving. When he goes further and recognises his sinfulness, he adds reparation to these three. But this attitude of mind is essentially humility. Therefore the ends for which Mass is offered are immediately an expression of humility. They imply a man's recognition of his own condition before God.

This would be true of any sacrifice. It is all the more true of the Mass, but the connection between the Mass and humility goes much further. We can sum it all up under the following heads. Firstly, at Mass we offer ourselves and all we have to God to do with us as he will. In other words, we put the " unprofitable-servant " principle into effect. Secondly, the Mass, as the sacrifice of Christ become our sacrifice too, is the only answer to the inadequacy of the creature before God. Thirdly, it enables us not alone to contemplate Our Lord in his supreme humiliation on the Cross, but it unites us with him in it, so that we don his humility and effectively reproduce his virtue in ourselves. Finally, the text of the Mass itself so constantly recalls to our attention that we are sinners and unworthy, that it must play a great part in bringing us gradually to a recognition of the fact. We will discuss each of these briefly.

At Mass, Christ offers us and himself to his Father. We must also offer him and ourselves. Otherwise our assistance at Mass is that of spectators and not of offerers. In doing so, we offer God the most holy dispositions of the soul of Christ and try to conform ourselves to them. These are adoration, gratitude, reparation for sin. Especially do we offer ourselves to the will of God. We tell him in effect that we are willing, as was his Son, to be obedient even unto death.

There will be little point, then, in offering ourselves to God at Mass in the morning with Christ, and during the day refusing to accept his will as it comes to us in the providential circumstances of our lives. This is particularly so when these circumstances are contrary and painful. In offering ourselves at Mass we are leaving ourselves open to a situation, the only adequate answer to which is the " unprofitable-servant " attitude, in which we summed up the practice of humility. Therefore, in offering ourselves at Mass we are doing something that imperatively demands humility. To live the Mass is to follow up the morning sacrifice with the repeated small acts of sacrifice of ourselves during the day. We may be called upon to sacrifice our time, our talents, our health, our leisure, or our ideas on work. Very likely we will be asked to accept the sacrifice of seeing all these taken from us. In virtue of our Mass-offering, we must give them gladly, freely, and completely. Otherwise, by our actions we deny the truth of our sacrifice. We tell Christ we are his and offer ourselves with him to the Father, and then in act refuse to let him take the offering. If humility can be resumed in the attitude of the unprofitable servant, the Mass is the source of our inspiration and strength for this attitude which it also indeed demands. Therefore, the offering of Mass is so closely connected with growth in humility as to be inseparable from it.

It will not be possible to unite ourselves sincerely with Christ at Mass and then refuse ourselves to him during the day. It must be expected that we shall find it hard. " I will not offer holocaust free-cost," said David to Areuna the Jebusite. So too with us, our sacrifice will cost us something. The dearer the thing we are called upon to give or relinquish, the nearer we are to him who was obedient unto death. It is unlikely that this latter will be asked of us. What we shall have to give will be the small repeated deaths of every day, the dying to ourselves, to our ideas and plans and hopes, that is needed if we would die effectively to the old man and live unto God. This is the price of humility, and this is what humility will do to us.

For it will remind us that, no matter what we give to God, we are still unprofitable servants.

After the Offertory we pray God to " accept our sacrifice in a spirit of humility and a contrite heart." Here we have the two basic dispositions for offering ourselves in sacrifice to God: humility, because we are creatures, and contrition, because we are sinners. But as the Mass demands these of us, so it increases them in us. This increase will be indirect, but it will be none the less real and substantial. It is really a matter of allowing ourselves to be reformed in mind and heart by the constantly renewed offering of all we have and are. Fidelity and sincerity are demanded of us. God's grace will bring about the rest.

There is more than this. The more we grow in humility, the greater will become our dependence and reliance on the Mass, in that it is the sacrifice of Christ. Faced with the task of worshipping God adequately, we are faced with the seemingly impossible. Between us and him there appears to yawn a gulf that we cannot cross. True, we cannot cross it by ourselves. But Christ the Bridge-Builder, the Pontifex, has crossed it and so made a way over it for us. This way, this bridge to God, is his sacrifice.

He gives us his own priestly act of offering to be ours. He gives us himself, the one completely adequate and worthy victim, to be ours also. By doing so he solves the problem of our inadequacy and poverty. He also delivers us from ourselves and the narrow prison of our littleness. We so become one with him that we are enabled to give all glory to God in the most adequate fashion. Alone we are poor and unable to worship God as we should. The capacity to do so was lost with sin, but the obligation remains. To the Mass, *the* sacrifice, we turn with relief and joy seeing in it, through Christ, the answer to our problem. But for this we must realise our need and incapacity. We must know that we are nothing of ourselves, and that only in Christ can we please the Father. But this is humility. Once again, it is a prerequisite and will itself be increased and strenghtened in us by the repetition of its own acts. To worship God adequately is not a problem for the humble soul, for its humility is the needed disposition for taking Christ's worship to itself. And the continued dependence on Christ demanded by the Mass will gradually liberate us from dependence on ourselves.

Can we go further and see something more in the Mass? Yes, we can. The Crucifixion was the great humiliation of Our Lord's life. It was the test of his obedience. He humbled himself becoming obedient even unto death, even to the death of the cross. His humility led him even as far as that.

In the Mass we are in contact with Christ in this, his supreme humiliation. It is not in his infancy, in his hidden life, or in his public mission, but on Calvary that Our Lord offers sacrifice. Betrayed, abandoned, mocked, he is delivered up to sinners and reputed a criminal. Apparently he has failed. This failure is his triumph, but none of that appeared on Calvary. And the same reality at which Mary and John looked on Calvary is before our eyes on the altar.

Therefore in uniting ourselves with him at Mass we are uniting ourselves with him in his humiliation. We are asking that we too be treated thus. As we have already seen, this is the merest justice for us, for we are sinners. He suffered all this for us. Made one with him, we cannot expect to be different. We cannot expect that all the suffering, all the humiliation, will be his and none of it ours. Otherwise, we are not really uniting ourselves with him on Calvary at all.

But we have already noted that it was not merely the humiliating circumstances of his death that constituted the humility of Christ. It was the disposition of his holy will which accepted these. Our humility is something internal too—a like disposition of soul. But where are we to get this if not in the Mass?

We contemplate him humiliated unto death. We unite ourselves with him, so that his dispositions may be reproduced in us. That we may become like him. That we may put on his mind. And we do this nowhere more truly than at Mass. For the Mass is effective through the graces we receive especially in Communion, in implanting these sentiments in us. To offer sacrifice with Christ, we not only need humility. We need his humility. And he gives us this in giving us himself at Mass, so that we are made one with him in soul and heart.

There is something else. If we allow the liturgy of the Mass to act on us, if we allow ourselves to become impregnated with the sentiments expressed in it, we will find it a marvellous instruction in true humility. For it constantly reminds us of what we are and of how unworthy we are. In it we are constantly brought back to the fact that we so readily forget—that we are sinners and are therefore unworthy to handle sacred things at all.

There is, for instance, the confession at the beginning of Mass, followed by the *Aufer a nobis*. Then, lest we should think ourselves cleansed, the eager, insistent petition of the repeated *Kyrie*, with its cry for mercy. Look at the *Munda cor meum*. Would it ever occur to any of us that we are unworthy even to read the Gospel, not to speak of offering the sacrifice of Christ? The kissing of the text after the Gospel—the very printed word of God is something holy.

These examples concern only the priest, but there is no reason why we should limit them to him exclusively. They are as applicable to those assisting as to the celebrant. We are all sinners, and all must offer the Mass. We all need these continual reminders of our unworthiness to do so. Go through the Mass and you will find a dozen such reminders of what we are, and of how unfit we are to handle things divine.

In order that the liturgical texts affect us this way, a great attention to them and a desire to profit from them is necessary. But granted this, daily assistance at Mass must gradually transform us. The constant confession of our unworthiness, the repeated cry for mercy, the reiterated request for cleansing, must inevitably humble us interiorly. You cannot repeatedly confess your unworthiness before God with sincerity and in a spirit of prayer, and not gradually come to realise it. You cannot say the *Munda cor meum* daily and not come to know that you are in truth a man of unclean lips. This transformation is not a mere matter of auto-suggestion. It will be a profound realisation, in faith and humility, of our sinfulness before God.

We have here dealt only with the Ordinary of the Mass, but the same principles apply to the Proper. For example, in the Mass for the third Sunday after Pentecost, the ideas of humility, poverty, dependence on God, sinfulness and forgiveness, the divine mercy, run right through every text. Praying these texts must induce and increase the corresponding dispositions in us.

But in this, as in all we have spoken of in this chapter, the influence will be largely indirect. It will happen of itself if you are attentive and sincere. All that is required is fidelity, not a conscious striving for effect, nor an eager looking for results from our prayers. As the repetition of acts forms a habit in us which is like a groove in our character, down which actions flow easily, so too with this. The repetition of the prayer formulae of the Mass if done with sincerity and devotion will wear a groove in the rock-ribbed hardness of our pride, down which will flow more easily the spiritual tears of true humility. But this must be left to God's grace. A too conscious effort to attain it will have the opposite effect. For it is difficult to watch yourself weep for your sins without becoming proud even of that. Rather contemplate Our Lord in his humility unto death, and so you will become like him.

CHAPTER XVIII

THE PROVIDENCE OF FAILURE

ONE of the facts of the spiritual life which we too often forget is that God seeks us as surely, as we seek him, and much more effectively. The quest for God that is the vocation of the Christian is itself a going forth to meet him as he comes to us. This is a powerful motive for hope and confidence, and should also condition our thinking on the subject of holiness.

We too readily regard holiness as exclusively the result of our own ascetic efforts. It is not that. Our asceticism must be directed to the removal of the obstacles so that God can enter. He says: Behold, I stand at the door and knock. Our task is to open the door. Then he will enter and will sup with us.

The matter is further obscured by the innate selfishness of our way of judging and thinking. Inevitably, when we consider the question of holiness as affecting ourselves and our own lives, we think of a holiness that is pleasing to ourselves. In theory we admit the need of the cross, of purification and of dying to ourselves. But in fact we see ourselves on the centre of the stage, even in our holiness and service of God. We imagine ourselves as objects of applause and commendation. We will be holy, we will serve God. Yes. But we shall thereby realise our dreams of fulfilling our personality and what is, in fact, our ego.

To think that this is not so is to be deficient in self-knowledge, and in a realisation of the extraordinary depths of egoism that are in all of us. In order to rid ourselves of these, our own efforts are not sufficient. The purifying action of God is needed, and all our lives should be a submission to this divine cleansing. Apart from any question of mystical purification, apart from any element of infused prayer or its concomitants, all life is a passion in a certain sense. It is an enduring of the sanctifying action of God.

This follows from what we said about holiness being a quest for us by God, as well as a quest for him by us. Because of this fact he in his Providence brings us to himself by the circumstances of our lives. If understood aright these circumstances are divine moulds shaping us to that likeness to himself that is the ideal fulfilment of our vocation.

Among these circumstances one of the most important is failure. Failure is an unpleasant word, and a more unpleasant reality. The ego flees from it. So does the world. But God uses it in our lives and he has a definite purpose in so doing. Its importance lies in the fact that if endured aright it has a transforming effect on us that few other comparable experiences have. This arises both from the nature of things, and from the ideal put before us by Christ in the Gospels.

Our Lord himself proclaimed the absolute law that life demands and pre-supposes death. Unless the grain of wheat falling into the ground die, it remains alone. But if it die, it brings forth much fruit. He reiterates the same thing in his other sayings about losing our life and gaining it unto eternity. In doing this he was not imposing an arbitrary demand from outside, an ascetic exercise which could be as well avoided or omitted. He was stating a profound necessity of man, considering his present state and his Christian vocation.

The grain of wheat must die. Otherwise it remains barren. But fruitfulness in the spirit for God is not merely spiritual activity or good works. It is something more than doing good to others; it is primarily and essentially holiness in ourselves. True holiness is fruitful to an extent that we do not understand. Holiness it is that makes us the fruitful branch of the Vine, and this being so, we must take it that God will do much towards our achievement of it. One of the principal means he will use is failure.

Failure can be considered necessary for our sanctification for three reasons. Firstly, in order that we be conformed to Christ; secondly, that we be rid of pride and self-sufficiency; and thirdly, that we be taught the supremely important lesson that God's will is its own justification. Let us explain each of these in turn.

First of all, conformity to Christ. This is our vocation and the life of Christ is the model and exemplar to which we must mould our own. Being members of his Body, we cannot expect that our lives will be different from his. They must bear on them the imprint of the Cross. In fact, it can be said that if they do not show signs of this, we can suspect that something is wrong, and that our lives are not as Christ-like as they should be.

But let us not make the mistake of thinking that the final failure of the Cross was the only failure in Our Lord's life. No, it was the culmination of a long succession of failures, dating from the very beginning of his ministry. He never, in fact, attained what we would consider success. He opened his public ministry by proclaiming himself the fulfilment of the prophetic words of Isaias: This day is fulfilled this Scripture in your ears. What was the reaction of the people—his people? Is not this Jesus, whose father and mother we know? This is no prophet, no Messias, this is only one of ourselves. And they thrust him out of the place.

That reaction seems almost to have set the pattern. So many came, so few believed. Among the most poignant scenes in all the gospel are surely those two where Our Lord is confronted with Philip's lack of understanding, and the shattered hopes of the disciples at Emmaus. Even with these, the closest ones, he had not succeeded. " So long a time, and you have not known me." " We hoped he would redeem Israel." Was this the only response his preaching and miracles could bring forth?

The failure of the cross seems to have cast a long shadow forward over the life of Our Lord, so that all he did shared in it in some way. Considering he was God, we would surely have looked for more from his preaching and his mission. Our ideas and ways are evidently not his. For it was through the failure of the cross that he triumphed. This moment of desolation and abandonment by all, of dereliction and disgrace, this was his hour. For this had he been born, for this had he come into the world. So that, looked at rightly, it seems rather that the repeated failures of his life were really foreshadowings of the great thing that was to come. Can we, being called to conformity, expect better? Is the disciple above the Master?

The second reason why failure is necessary is to rid us of self-sufficiency. Pride and egoism go so deep in us that their effects are almost endless. Only when we try to eradicate and uproot them do their devious ramifications come slowly, one by one, to light. There is nothing we cannot be proud of, and nothing to which we cannot put our name.

We know that nothing is ours. We know the truths about our dependence on God. We know that in him we live and are. But there is a difference between knowing these truths and realising them. It is the distinction made by Newman between notional and real assent. As well as knowing something we must realise it, if it is to be an effective source of action in our lives. Speculative knowledge will not ordinarily provide sufficient motivation to move us. Knowledge must be, to some extent at least, effective. It must be realised.

If we are to realise and be really conscious of our incapacity and inadequacy, we must experience them. We must feel them. They must be continually borne in on us by the tangible evidence of them that is failure. If the armour of our pride is to be pierced, if the subtlety of our ego is to be defeated, if the self is to be left completely naked and exposed in its native helplessness, failure is needed. Nothing else is so effective, and nothing else will show us so convincingly that we are in very truth dependent on God.

Despite our best efforts, therefore, we must expect failure. Not only that, but when it comes we must not be discouraged by it, but see in it the loving hand of God, freeing us from the prison of our self-sufficiency.

The final reason why failure is necessary is to teach us to do God's will for its own sake. We might think that this is something so evidently desirable in itself, that we would do it easily and of ourselves. But we do not. We all of us work for results. We do not perhaps recognise the aim of our strivings as success. But we want to see our work issue in results which will gratify us and bring commendation or notice to us. We can do this even in the pursuit of holiness. But to work for results is not the same as to do God's will.

This attitude of mind is due partly to our criterion of success, which is precisely results. It is due partly to our pride, which cannot abide our works appearing sterile. But if we succeed along these lines, it is greatly to be feared that we will arrive at the end of life without any real change within ourselves. God has given us this life for one purpose, that is to prepare for the vision of him hereafter. This means that he expects us to use life to bring about a radical

7

change within ourselves. This change involves principally that we learn to do his will because it is his will. That is holiness. Anything else is a form of self-seeking. We do not say that it is sinful, but it is selfish. And it will not sanctify us, however excellent be the results we achieve in the way of conversions, alms given, needs of others supplied.

Unless we are changed in ourselves, we risk arriving at the end of life with empty hands, and being told by Christ that we have had our reward. But the urge to work for results and success is so strong and deep in us that the powerful action of God is needed to uproot the tendency. The divine intervention which has the most far-reaching results will be failure. If, despite our best efforts, we several times fail in what we are doing, we must inevitably either abandon everything or become detached from the results.

As the first reaction is evidently that of pique and chagrin, we shall avoid it if we are sincere. The second, therefore, detachment, will happen almost despite ourselves. We shall be forced to revise our standards and ideas of success. We shall see that it is quite evident from providential circumstances that God does not want results, but the service of our submission to his will. We shall gradually realise that this alone is important. It is likewise all we can give God that is our own. We cannot do anything for him that cannot be done better by someone else. No result is so necessary to him that our work must be considered to have failed if we do not achieve it.

These ideas are forced in on our awareness, and there is slowly born the realisation that God's standards and ours are different. And as his are right, ours are wrong. He wants our service, our love, our life to be offered to him and left in his hands. That is all. But that means, in practice, doing things because they are his will, not because we want to do them, or because they will issue in satisfying results. The issue of anything we do is God's affair. Ours is simply to do it. To be convinced of this is to be very near to holiness. And nothing can compare with failure for begetting and fostering this conviction in us. When we constantly fail to get results, they cease to matter and to occupy our attention.

There is here a danger that must be avoided. If failure can be so excellent, it is desirable. Should we not, therefore, seek it rather than success? No, definitely not. Failure is not desirable in itself. It is desirable only as a means of purification, and is useful only if and in so far as we allow ourselves to be conditioned by it. We must submit to it. It must happen to us. It must, therefore, be providential. Otherwise, it is not the hand of God, but our own. To seek failure would in some sense involve a contradiction. If we were to seek it, we would most likely be seeking ourselves, and would so render it useless. God can, in fact, be glorified by our success, and can be equally well served by it as by our failure. But our condition is such that he will use failure to bring about a definite condition of soul in us, which can hardly be attained by any other means. Or at least not so effectively. But this action is his, and must be left to him.

Therefore we must work for success, while being at the same time quite detached from it. To seek failure would very likely deprive us of initiative and incentive and so eventually render us unwilling to work at all. To seek failure could also be a subtle form of escape from the responsibilities of work, and so become a cloak for laziness or incompetence. We must act as though everything depended on ourselves, but realise that everything depends on God. Therefore when failure providentially comes, we must see in it the hand of God lovingly stretched out, not over our works but over our souls, that he might draw us to himself.

In what particular sphere of activity may we expect failure? In almost any. It may be in our efforts to acquire some virtue, to eradicate a fault,[1] or something which, though not sinful, is holding us back. It may be in our personal relations with others, in our attempts to influence others, to teach them, to change their thought and outlook. Failure can meet us in the attempt to advance in mental prayer, or the continued daily struggle with the same temptations and difficulties. Sickness may render us unfit for work, or our incapacity may cause a project to founder. We can fail in the secrecy of our own heart, or in the humiliating limelight of the public eye. Others may praise us while we ourselves know that we have failed, or success being ours may be found to be bitter in our mouths. Perhaps all the world looks on us as having failed, and says of us what was said at Emmaus: We had hoped. Failure may come to us as a continued lack of recognition, or repeated misunderstanding, or the unwillingness of others to use our talents.

Whatever it be, however it comes, there is a providence in it.

---

[1] See what was said in Chapter VI about God allowing sins in order to cure pride.

It is the action of God likening us to his Son, purifying us of pride, teaching us his will. Properly understood and rightly submitted to, there are few merely natural circumstances in our lives that are as sanctifying as failure. In order that this be realised, we must accept it with humility, and this acceptance is itself a unique means of growth in the virtue.

CHAPTER XIX

HE MUST INCREASE

Our discussion of the humility of Our Lord showed us that it consisted in great measure of the acceptance of failure. Failure met him all during his life and he finally died in what seemed to be the very apogee of failure on the cross. This was his triumph, but that did not appear on Calvary.

In St. John the Baptist we find a humility that is concerned with the opposite—with success. St. John was a saint who found his works and preaching crowned with remarkable success, and who never let this affect him. It is true that in the end he died miserably in the dungeons at Macherus, the victim of a drunken king's vanity, " because of those who were with him and because of his promise " to a dancing girl. But that end in obscurity before seeing his preaching flower into the Messianic Kingdom is itself of a piece with the remainder of his life. It is surely what the humility of St. John would have sought. The loneliness and isolation of Macherus, the solitariness of the saint in the death-cell, his disciples unaware of his fate until after it was over—it all fits in.

In contrast to Our Lord's birth, John's beginnings could not have appeared ordinary to those who knew him. He was born when his parents were already old and when Elizabeth could no longer expect motherhood. He was a child of promise from the beginning. His father was struck dumb from the time of the child's conception until his birth. The family and friends sought to name him for one of his forebears, but Zachary announced: " His name is John." A child sent by God and named by God. A child of prodigy and of portent. So that when he was born the tongue of Zachary was not only loosed but was so inspired that he could foretell: " And thou, child, shalt be called the prophet of the Most High, for thou shalt go before the ways of the Lord, to give knowledge of salvation to his people." No wonder those assembled in the home of Elizabeth looked at each other in astonishment and said one to another: " What a one think you shall this child be ? " For everyone could see that the hand of God was on him.

The gospels tell us nothing of the early life of John. We can take it that he did not go out into the desert before young manhood. But we can be quite certain that none of the incidents surrounding his birth were forgotten. If anything, they would be added to by the villagers. When the child of promise left his home and went out into the wilderness, heads were shaken and nods were exchanged, and surely they must have said: " We knew it, for the hand of God was on him. Do you remember the time he was born ? " For these things were spoken of in all the hill-country about.

All this is important in that it set the stage for his re-appearance as the preacher from the desert. As a prophet he was in the very best tradition. As one whom the people could respect and follow, he started off under the most favourable auspices. It is difficult to imagine a sequence of circumstances in early life which would better have stamped John with the rôle of teacher, and which therefore prepared, not himself, but the people, for his mission. They could not say of him as they said of Christ: " Is not this the carpenter whose brethren are here with us ? " They expected great things of John. They expected that he would speak as one having power, that he would denounce evil and call them to better things.

His appearance by Jordan bank fulfilled their fearful hopes. Hope they had, for his coming was a sign that there was yet a prophet in Israel. But their hope was tempered with fear, for this man from the desert would blast their hypocrisy and their shallowness. He came as another Elias—his hair unshorn, his loins girt with camel cloth, his limbs spare and gaunt from fasting, his skin burnt by the fierce Judean sun, and like a veritable prophet indeed began: " Ye offspring of vipers, who hath shown you to flee from the wrath that is to come ? . . . "

John must have had a powerful effect on the Jews. That he attracted them to his baptism of penance in great numbers is clear from the gospels. Such a one as he could not but attract. The fire of his preaching, the miracles at the time of his birth, now retold anew, the holiness and the austerity of his life, the mystery and the strange allure that the desert and its dwellers always have; all these contributed to make the Baptist a power and a centre of attraction. Placed against the background of the Roman occupation this is all the more true. For he would, even without his intending it, have revived the flagging nationalistic hopes of the people. In him they would inevitably have seen the possibility of revival for the Jewish nation.

This, however, would be merely accidental. The great factor in the success of his mission would be the fact that he was a man sent by God to bear witness. God would therefore bless his efforts and they would be fruitful. God had raised him up in order that he might preach repentence to the people. He was to recall the Jews to fervour in their religion. This mission was divine and therefore it must succeed.

We are not left to conjecture in this. That it would be a great mistake to consider John as influencing only a small group of disciples is shown conclusively by the evidence of two witnesses, St. Luke and Josephus.

In the eighteenth chapter of *Acts*, St. Luke tells us of Apollo, an Alexandrian, " an eloquent man and one mighty in the Scriptures." He is a rather mysterious figure, who was preaching the gospel in Ephesus and at Corinth. " He was fervent in spirit and he spoke and taught the things concerning Jesus." But strangely enough, he knew only the baptism of John. It is odd that knowing so much of Christ, he did not know his baptism. But what concerns us here is that he did know that of John. Here was a man preaching what was, to some extent, a form of " Baptist " Christianity throughout Asia Minor and Greece. There is nothing local about such discipleship or influence. The case of the twelve disciples of Ephesus, whose story is told in the next chapter of *Acts*, was much the same. Fervent believers, apparently, but convinced that John had the fulness of the message. " He was not the light but was sent to give testimony of the light." But the Ephesians thought he was the light.

Josephus gives added evidence of John's influence. He says: " Many came in crowds around him (John) and were moved by his words. Herod feared that the great influence of John might put it into his head to raise a rebellion, for the people seemed ready to do whatever he said. Herod preferred, therefore, to ensure his own personal safety by preventing any mischief John might do; rather than by leaving him free, to give himself cause to regret it afterwards. Accordingly because of Herod's suspicions he was sent a prisoner to Macherus . . . and there put to death." [1]

It is easy enough to reconcile this with St. Mark who says that Herod imprisoned John because of Herodias. The king would have reason to fear that the Baptist's public denunciations of his adultery might lead the mob to attempt to dethrone him. He might fear it more because John was preaching the coming of the Messias, and could well believe, and therefore suggest to the crowd, that the conversion of the king was a necessary prelude to the reign of justice. It would be an easy step from that to having some fanatic in the preacher's audience reason that if the king were not converted, he must be removed. Anyhow, whatever we make of the passage from the Jewish historian, it points to a great influence over the people on the part of the Baptist.

Here we have the ideal situation making for self-assertion. A successful leader and speaker, with powerful influence over others —such a one is inevitably faced with the temptation to draw others to himself, instead of directing them onwards. To remain completely and effectively in the background, while still influencing those who come to him, demands rare virtue indeed. It imperatively demands that he appreciate clearly that his function is of one who passes. He must direct men beyond himself. He must point the way and see those he directs pass him by as they would a sign-post.

There are few who are capable of this. To be a leader and yet not lead. To be a success, but only for the sake of someone else. To influence others on a great, even a national or international scale, but only to point out to them him who was yet to come. To march at the head of a people, only in order to hand them over to another leader. And not only to do this, but to be consumed by the will to do it. To realise to the full the tremendous responsibility of being only a sign-post, ever pointing onwards.

All this was fulfilled in John. He described himself as a voice. Not an apostle, nor a prophet nor even a servant of the Messias. But a voice in the wilderness—his only desire being that men might hear, and hearing him, go on to Jesus. His mission was so much

---

[1] *Jewish Antiquities*, Bk. 18, Ch. 5.

more important than himself that he had completely forgotten himself. It never occurred to him that others would not do the same. Is there anything more clear in the gospels than this? And they sent to him to ask him: Who art thou? Art thou the Christ? Or Elias? Or the prophet? To all of which John answered: No, I am not. I am a voice crying in the wilderness. But there comes one after me, the latchet of whose shoe I am not worthy to loose.

This incident at first sight appears simple enough. John was asked who he was, and he gave the answer that he was not the Messias. But not only were the people ready to believe, they wanted to believe that this was the Messias. He was in the best tradition of Israel, a man of God come in from the desert. He had the loyalty and the obedience of the people—at a word they would follow him anywhere. Their esteem for him was such that after his death, when Jesus asked Peter: Whom do men say that I am?—Peter could answer: Some say John the Baptist. This was the greatest figure that occurred to them. They could not imagine one greater than John. And when Herod heard of Our Lord's fame and the miracles he wrought, he thought the same. And the king said: " John, whom I beheaded, is risen again from the dead, and therefore mighty works show themselves in him." Greater esteem can hardly be imagined. The people wanted to be told he was the Christ, they took him to be Christ, and they were ready to believe in his resurrection from the dead.

John the Baptist therefore had power—power such as is given to few men. He had that sweetest and most tempting kind of power—ability to lead others where he would. In this he had in his hands the possibility even of sabotaging Christ's mission, and so jeopardising the whole work of Redemption. Is this thought fantastic? Why should it be? Other men, before and since John, have come as instruments and thought they were principals. Others have been asked to play second fiddle and have wanted to conduct. Others have drawn souls to themselves instead of to God.

Imagine what would have happened had John told the delegation from Jerusalem that he was the Christ. They would have hailed him as the Deliverer, would more than likely have raised the banner of national freedom under his leadership, would have hung on his slightest word and wish. We must not think this was impossible, that John could not be tempted. As we said in speaking of Our Lord, we must constantly remind ourselves that all the events of his life worked themselves out as do those of all our lives. He was as subject to circumstances as we are. Making due allowance for his holiness and his mission, the Baptist could be tempted. Indeed according to the laws of the spiritual life, the greater his sanctity and mission the greater would be his temptation. The keener the tempering required the more intense the fire into which the steel is plunged.

And this temptation is one that would not trouble a lesser man. It is a temptation of the strong, of the great. It was one of the temptations of Christ. It was as we have seen the only one of Our Lord's temptations that was repeated. " Show thyself that all may believe in thee! " The Precursor would not be above the Master, and temptation would strike him too.

In his long years in the desert John must have fought with temptation many times. The desert is traditionally the abode of the devil. Among the barren rocks of the Judean wilderness, where the Baptist retired at night after his days spent in preaching and baptising, the demon would be waiting for him. The whisper would come: " Art thou the Christ, or he that is to come? " And the future of the Kingdom, the revelation of the Messias, the closing of the old era and the opening of the new, depended on the answer of this one man. Should he fail, all would be lost. Should he forget that most difficult of truths, that he himself was no one but only pointed to a greater, then the very coming of that greater one would be in danger.

But John did not forget. He did not fail. He rose magnificently to the heights of his vocation, which paradoxically demanded that he sink to the depths of nothingness. " For I am not the Christ . . . I should be baptised by him . . . I am not worthy to loose his shoe . . . He must increase, but I must decrease."

That is why we said that the circumstances of his death did not really matter. Once Christ had come and manifested himself in the Jordan, John's task was over. His mission was ended and he himself must decrease until eventually he would be lost sight of altogether. And the dungeons of Macherus were as good a place as any for that. What did it matter now what happened him? If he vanished into the wilderness beyond the Dead Sea and died there in isolation, his humility would accept that. He had no further work to do. He must decrease and disappear. It was not his to see his work crowned. Not his to see the issue of his preaching

—the Messianic Kingdom, the early Church. He had sown and others would reap. His humility lay in knowing that. Christ said of him that greater had not been born. In this lay true greatness— that he could withdraw and become little again, giving way to another who came after him. And it was his humility that enabled him to sum up, not only his mission, but all spiritual life: He must increase, I must decrease.

CHAPTER XX

THE HUMILITY
OF HIS HANDMAID

T HE humility of Our Lady, like her holiness, is so great that we cannot comprehend it. Not only does it pervade all she does, casting its fragrance over all her life, but it is itself the very reason for God's choice of her.

"Had Mary not been humble the Spirit of the Lord would not have rested on her. But if he had not rested on her he would certainly not have made her fruitful. For how could she have conceived by him without his co-operation? It is clear then that, as she herself tells us, God regarded the humility of his handmaid, rather than her virginity, in order that she might conceive by the Holy Ghost. So although she was pleasing on account of her virginity, it was her humility that made her a mother. And so it may be said that her humility was the true reason why the Lord took complacence in her virginity." [1]

It must not be thought that this is mere rhetoric, the permissible exaggeration of the preacher. No, it expresses a profound and mysterious truth. As she sings her *Magnificat*, Mary is the holiest of creatures. She is something else also. She is the poorest, and between these two there is a close and necessary connection. For she is the epitome of all the yearnings and the hopes and the longings of Israel for the Messias. God's poor have awaited his

[1] St. Bernard, *Sermon* 1 *on the Glories of the Virgin Mother*.

coming—and their sentiments and hopes are summed up in Mary. She is at the apex of a triangle, at the base of which are the promises made to Abraham and the Fathers. She will not only long for Christ but will herself bring him into the world.

God became man for all men, but in a particular way for her who was to be his mother. He came in response to the desire and prayers of the holy ones of the Old Testament, but especially in response to the prayers of Mary. For the holiness of all the just men of old is a flickering candle beside the strong shining of the sun of Mary's justice. According as her sanctity was the greater, so was the Incarnation more for her.

But all this was because of her humility. She says so herself in the *Magnificat*: He hath done great things to me because he hath regarded the humility of his handmaid. She offered God nothing else but this, that she was completely and perfectly poor in spirit. So perfect was her poverty that she would possess not only the Kingdom, but the King himself. And she would so possess him that he would depend on her for life and would belong to her as a child belongs to its mother. God could come no nearer to a creature than this.

The humility of Our Lady was no mere matter of not being proud. It was, in a sense, impossible that she should be proud. Recall the words of St. John of the Cross, which we quoted earlier about the soul's progress in humility. As soon as it begins to make progress at all it becomes so enlightened as to its unworthiness before God that it never occurs to it that it is better than others. The saint is here talking about a very elemenatry degree of the spiritual life—the beginning of the night of the senses. There is nothing extraordinary or rare about it. It is the first step in holiness.

If this is so for the rest of us, what effect must the surpassing holiness of Mary have had on her evaluation of herself? Her sanctity is so great that it exceeds that of all the angels and saints together. No one under God, says Pius IX, can comprehend it. She simply could not, then, be proud. God did not choose her because her humility showed him that she would not abuse his gifts and use them for self-glorification. Indeed, the expression of such a thought about Our Lady is itself sufficient to show how inadequate and almost irreverent is its very suggestion. Virtue that is a mere avoiding of its opposite vice may be all we are capable of. But it has no place in the soul of the Immaculate One.

Her virtue is a deep and essential thing. It is a positive and powerful force, uniting her with God and placing her utterly beyond temptation's breath. Her humility is something almost elemental. It springs from a profound and vivid reverence for God and an understanding, not of her sinfulness, for she had no sin, but of her lowly condition in the presence of him who was all. Our Lord told Catherine of Sienna to realise that he was and that she was not. " I am he who is, thou art she who is not". But those words had been said to Mary long before. They had echoed in the silence of her immaculate soul at its conception—they re-echoed in her pure and virginal heart at the coming of God in the Incarnation, and they re-echoed again in her *Magnificat*, that very battle-hymn of humility.

Mary's sense of the divine was unique and great. It was as great as was her sanctity. So too was her sense of her own lowliness before God. The self-knowledge of any saint, his sense of unworthiness and of God's greatness, pales into insignificance beside the humility of Mary. Our Lady's humility is the very perfection of the poverty that cries out, " Jesus, Son of David, have mercy." It is the abyss of poverty calling to the abyss of divine goodness and pity. It is the hunger of the crowd, hungry for redemption, that must be satisfied by the coming of the Living Bread. It is the yearning and the longing and the hope, the need and the desire of every heart, summed up in the pure heart of the Virgin of Nazareth. Such poverty could be enriched only by the coming of God himself. So he filled the hungry with good things and sent away the rich empty. He received Israel and remembered his mercy. As though the cry of Mary's heart recalled it to him. Having promised the Father of believers, he would fulfil the promise to Our Lady, for in her he found the perfect receptivity, the complete emptiness, the readiness for him that was perfect poverty and humility.

In discussing the question as to why God did not become incarnate at the beginning of the human race, immediately after the Fall, St. Thomas has this to say: " The Lord did not bestow upon the human race the remedy of the Incarnation at the beginning, lest they should despise it through pride, if they did not already recognise their disease." Man had to feel his need of God. It had to be brought home to him by the palpable experience of his own inadequacy. If they were to be saved, men had to realise their need of salvation and their inability to save themselves. Otherwise they would receive the Saviour with contempt, saying, " We have no need of you."

It is not fanciful then to see God as awaiting, down the ages, the soul who would be truly poor in spirit. The one who would know and be aware of its own poverty and lowliness and to whom, therefore, he could give everything, even himself. In the Patriarchs and Prophets and the holy men before Christ, there was indeed poverty and a realisation of the need for God. But in Mary it culminated and reached perfection. Not that she must feel her indigence by her imperfection, for of this she had none. But that God would so grace her that she would know it of herself.

Knowing our need by experiencing it is, after all, only a second best. Knowing our littleness by knowing God is the ideal. And in Mary God restored the pristine order of creation before sin entered and distorted man's vision of God and himself. She saw God. She saw herself as a reflection of God, as an effect of his goodness —and her soul magnified him. Before she sang the words of her *Magnificat*, the accents of her holy soul had sung them in the secrecy of her intimacy with God. And God replied to them by coming to her with the gift of himself: He hath regarded the humility of his handmaid and hath done great things to me.

This humility of Our Lady sheds a gracious light of modesty over all her life and suffuses her actions with a sense of reverence before the mystery of God. Faced with the difficult and trying fulfilment of the census order of Cyrinus, she bowed to God's Providence and went to Bethlehem—so that the prophecies might be fulfilled. Though she was the holier, Joseph was the head of the Holy Family and of the home at Nazareth. To him the angel came at night with the warning to fly into Egypt. To him he came again with the command to return to Nazareth.

The Presentation in the Temple furnishes us with a shining example of Our Lady's humility. Mary approaches the Temple, the dwelling place of God with men. But as she does, the Child whom she carries in her arms is the fulfilment of all that the Temple signified—for now at last the Lord is come to his Temple in very truth. He is the fulfilment of the law, the desired of all nations, the Messias. She who carries him is the holiest of creatures, the only child of Adam who never needed, nor could need, any Purification. Yet to look at them none of this is apparent.

A very ordinary Jewish mother and her child are coming up the
Temple steps to carry out the precept of the Law. Every male child
must be offered to God, and every mother must be purified after
the days are accomplished. Does Mary even think of refusing to
go to the Temple? Does she claim to be above the Law, to have
no need, as indeed she had not, of purification, just as her Son,
God's only-begotten, had no need of being offered to his Father?
No, she acts like all the other young mothers who doubtless were
also there that morning. Surely we have here the very apogee of
" Love to be unknown." She is in very deed unknown. A poor
mother, the wife of an artisan. She does not even stand out from
the others as wealthy. She offers the two doves of the poor. There
is in this gesture a depth of meaning that is lost to those around.
Not only was she poor, but she was God's Poor One. The priests
think she is no one, those about take no notice of her. Yet she is
Queen of Heaven and second only to her Divine Son.

And when Simeon takes the child and speaks of his greatness,
does she eagerly interrupt and assure him that she knows? Not a
word is recorded from her. She listens reverently to Simeon and
keeps silence, keeping all these things in her heart. What a marvellous picture—and how different from our way of acting! How we
will parade our virtues, our qualities, our talents, our relationship
with the great ones of the world, our achievements—anything that
will give us a little superiority! How few, even spiritual persons,
are willing to be unknown and esteemed as nothing! How seldom
we will allow those to instruct us whom we consider our inferiors.
But how inferior to Mary were not Simeon and Anna! How ready
are we to criticise others—how does not the silence of Mary here
rebuke us! This whole incident breathes a reverence for God and
his works that is hardly paralleled elsewhere.

You meet it all through Mary's life—the sense of her being
constantly silent in the face of the mysterious workings of God's
Providence. There is the finding in the Temple. Her gentle
question: Son, why did you do this? Then to Our Lord's reply—
her silence. The Father's business was the unfolding of his plan
for the salvation of men. And Mary was silent in face of it. Her
silence is not one of hurt or incomprehension. It is the silence
begotten of reverence, that overtakes the holy soul in presence of
God. It is the direct fruit of a practical sense of the divine.

All these incidents are bathed in the light of the *Magnificat*.

Its sentiments permeate the whole life and all the actions of Our Lady, because they express the essential attitude of her soul.

The *Magnificat* has a further lesson. Our Lady did not take the glory to herself, but neither did she fail to recognise the gifts of God in herself. We said earlier that humility is not a matter of having a low opinion of oneself or one's gifts. This brings it out clearly and unmistakeably. Mary saw all that God hath done for her, and sang of it: He hath done great things to me. But it was all only a further motive for her to glorify God, to adore him in self-forgetfulness. She could look with equanimity on the fact that all generations would call her blessed, and find therein only a reason for glorifying God. That is real humility—where the soul becomes so pure and selfless that it perfectly reflects the Creator.

This is the ideal of humility: " That we should magnify God who works in us and not be elated by our virtues." (St. Benedict). Not being afraid to do good because of pride or fearing to acknowledge the effects of God's love for us, but simply to give him all the glory.

In Our Lady, then, we have a perfect model, and in her *Magnificat* a profound expression of true humility. She is the greatest and the least, the mightiest and the humblest of creatures—and she knows it.

" Who is this virgin so venerable that she is saluted by an angel, so humble that she is espoused to an artisan . . . Surely that soul must be highly pleasing to God in which humility commends virginity and virginity adorns humility. Of what degree of reverence shall we not judge her to be worthy, whose humility fruitfulness glorifies, and whose virginity is consecrated by motherhood? You have learned that she is a virgin and you have learned that she was humble. If you cannot imitate her virginity, at least imitate her humility. Desirable as is virginity, humility is more necessary. The former is counselled but the latter is commanded. To the one we are invited, to the other obliged . . . If therefore you can only admire the virginity of Mary, apply yourself zealously to copy her humility and that will be enough for you." [2]

[2] St. Bernard, *Sermon* 1 *on the Glories of the Virgin Mother.*

✠ M. H. GILL AND SON LIMITED, PRINTERS, DUBLIN.